PRACTICAL DICTATION AND TRANSCRIPTION

SHORTERHAND EDITION

**Stenography and Transcription Training
for Today's Business**

By
DOROTHY F. HAYDON
ELAYNE GORDON

Edited by Marion Angus

Distributed by
LAIDLAW BROTHERS
A Division of Doubleday & Company, Inc.
River Forest, Illinois

Pitman Publishing Corporation
6 East 43rd Street, New York, N.Y. 10017

Dorothy F. Haydon, B.B.A., M.S. in Education, is former Chairman of Secretarial Studies Department, George Washington High School, New York, New York, and an adjunct faculty member of Pace University, New York, New York.

Elayne Gordon, B.S. in Education, M.A., is Assistant Principal of Business Education Department, Newtown High School, Elmhurst, New York.

Marion Angus, P.C.T., F.S.C.T., C.S.R., is a Business Education Consultant, Editor, and Lecturer for the Pitman Company. Her lectures in business education are given at all levels—students, teachers, colleges, universities, seminars, etc.

PITMAN PUBLISHING CORPORATION
6 East 43rd Street, New York, N.Y. 10017, U.S.A.

PITMAN PUBLISHING
COPP CLARK PUBLISHING
517 Wellington Street West, Toronto, Canada M5V 1G1

SIR ISAAC PITMAN AND SONS LTD.
Pitman House, Parker Street, Kingsway, London WC2B 5PB
P.O. Box 46038, Banda Street, Nairobi, Kenya

SIR ISAAC PITMAN (AUST.) PTY. LTD.
Pitman House, 158 Bouverie Street, Carlton, Victoria 3053, Australia

Library of Congress Cataloging in Publication Data

Haydon, Dorothy F
    Practical dictation and transcription.

    SUMMARY: A training program for basic stenog-
raphy and transcription utilizing realistic letters
from modern business offices.
    1. Shorthand--Pitman. [1.   Shorthand--Pitman]
I. Gordon, Elayne, joint author. II. Title.
Z56.H377 1975   653'.424   75-14357
ISBN 0-273-01021-2

Manufactured in the United States of America

1. 0 9 8 7 6 5 4 3 2 1

TO THE STUDENT:

Transcription is a composite skill, made up of other skills which you have already partially developed. These skills are the ability to write and read shorthand notes, the ability to typewrite, and the ability to spell and punctuate in good English form. By combining these skills, you learn to transcribe.

Accuracy is the most important working asset of a stenographer. Although reasonable speed is essential, speed without accuracy often results in the loss of valuable time. In your transcription work, therefore, strive for accuracy. Always proofread your work before you remove it from the typewriter.

Hints for Improving Your Shorthand:

1. Use two standard shorthand notebooks: one for home practice and the other for class dictation.
2. Keep your outlines neat and controlled.
3. Write correct shorthand.
4. Use proper writing tools at all times.
5. Review the pacers, intersections, and phrases regularly.
6. Practice, writing in stenography, material found in newspapers, books, and magazines. Read the plate material and your "cold" notes as frequently as you can. The faster you are able to read your notes, the faster you will be able to write from dictation.
7. Always write with good posture.

Hints for Improving Your Typing:

1. Try to practice from printed copy at least 10 minutes daily.
2. Transcribe pacers and phrases to develop facility at the typewriter.
3. Do corrective work to eliminate repeated typing errors.
4. Use good typing techniques at the typewriter.
5. Use the speed devices on your typewriter.

Proofreading:

1. Everything you type must be proofread.
2. Pick the method you like best and use it all the time. (Your teacher will discuss methods of proofreading with you.)
3. Follow the context as you proofread. If you understand the letter it will help you to avoid errors in tense, number, and usage.

Transcription Aids:

1. Date your notebook each day at the bottom of the page.
2. Cancel your transcribed notes as you complete them.
3. Use a rubber band to separate used from unused pages.
4. Make a note of enclosures or special notations, in red, before you begin to type.
5. Use identifying initials on each letter.
6. Make all corrections neatly so that the finished product is clean and attractive in appearance.
7. Use your dictionary to verify and correct spelling and syllabication.

Preface

TO THE TEACHER:

Practical Dictation and Transcription presents a well-organized training program to help the pupil develop the integrated skills necessary for successful notetaking and transcription.

There are twenty chapters in the text, each of which contains five units. These units provide extensive *teaching* and *practice* material. In addition there are, in the Teacher's Key, six test letters after every two chapters: these letters test knowledge application and will be a great help in the evaluation of the progress of the pupils. They will also indicate clearly, where remedial work is needed.

Objectives:

1. To strengthen the pupil's knowledge of the principles of Pitman stenography.
2. To develop the ability to write common words and business terms, phrases, and contracted forms, in context; and to develop the ability to initiate outlines for unfamiliar words while taking dictation.
3. To develop the ability to sustain dictation.
4. To broaden the pupil's business background through dictation and transcription of business letters classified according to many areas of business and industry.
5. To learn how to apply correlated knowledge (spelling, punctuation, grammar, business information and business usage) to the production of accurate transcripts.

Format:

The VOCABULARY BUILDER section provides illustrations of the principles stressed in each unit and can be used as a reading drill, a writing drill, and/or a recall drill. It serves at the same time as a preview for the letters that follow in the chapter. Thus, vocabulary that has been *reviewed* and *previewed* is applied immediately in context. Additional vocabulary that occurs in the letters provides an opportunity for initiation of similar words.

Homonyms in English and stenographic outlines having distinguishing features are introduced to the pupils under the heading SPECIAL OUTLINES. In addition, a punctuation or transcription aid is included in each unit under the caption TRANSCRIPTION POINTER. These items are also applied in the letters which make up the chapter.

The content of the letters is of particular interest. The letters are derived from the work of modern business offices and each chapter introduces the student to current usage in style and language in a different field. The letters are varied in length and difficulty to provide a variety of dictation experiences for the learner at every stage. These letters apply the outlines presented in the VOCABULARY BUILDER. Other technical vocabulary and important phrases are previewed before each letter. The CHALLENGE LETTER which completes each unit provides material for high-speed dictation and an opportunity for practice in the recall of frequently-used words and phrases. Here again, the high points of the unit are included for overall application.

The letters have been syllabically counted so that dictation is controlled at an intensity of 1.4. This makes it possible to include more technical letters without making the vocabulary count too difficult.

The topical grouping of the letters provides for enrichment of instruction through correlation with business terms and practices. Some business terms are defined; for others, questions are provided for the pupil to answer. It is hoped that pupils will be encouraged to use reference books as well as a dictionary. Principal cities and states, as well as some foreign countries, are previewed systematically and presented in the inside addresses or as part of the letter content. A wide variety of proper names are included so that the pupil can develop skill in writing names when they occur in dictation.

TEST LETTERS are an additional part of the Teacher's Key. Six test letters are provided after every two chapters; the content is based upon the materials in the chapters. The teacher is able to test the pupils, therefore, on what they have been practicing and studying in the preceding ten units. The teacher can choose those letters which seem most suitable to the needs of the class.

Table of Contents

CHAPTER   PAGE

1.	Advertising	1
2.	Printing and Publishing	21
3.	Basic Industries	41
4.	Fashion	61
5.	Apology, Complaint, Adjustment, Appreciation	81
6.	Travel and Transportation	101
7.	Banking	121
8.	Office and Home Furnishings	141
9.	Education, Schools, On-the-job Training	161
10.	Review	181
11.	Finance	201
12.	Entertainment	221
13.	Hobbies	241
14.	Law	261
15.	Shipping	282
16.	Insurance	301
17.	Machinery and Equipment	320
18.	Real Estate	340
19.	Employment	358
20.	Review	378

1

Advertising

UNIT 1

VOCABULARY BUILDER

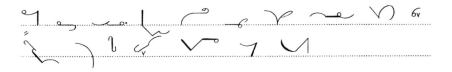

Key

Sunday section enclosing department locations excellent earliest magazine policy slight problem order drive while bargains enjoy variety

SPECIAL OUTLINES

available................valuable................

available means ready for use; utilizable.
valuable means having money value; precious.
  Credit will not be *available* to you if you do not pay your bills.
  The assets of the business are *valuable* in obtaining credit.

TRANSCRIPTION POINTER

  Good paragraphing is an essential part of a business letter. A paragraph generally represents a distinct subdivision dealing with a particular point of the subject. Good paragraphing is an aid to clarity and understanding.

1

When you prepare your notes for transcription you should indicate where the new paragraphs will begin by placing a double diagonal line at the paragraph points: //

1

Hobart .... Randall .... Miami .... Florida ....

Christmas .... at that time .... please let us know ....

to receive attention .... similar ....

, 308 , 9 , , 33107

2

Fuller .... Causeway .... Jacksonville .... single ....

telephone ....

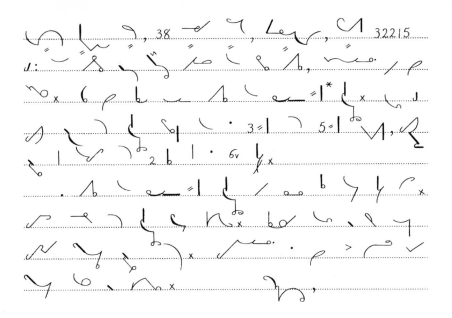

3

Bay Shore .... Daytona Beach .... clearance ....

at this time .... sportswear .... merchandise ....

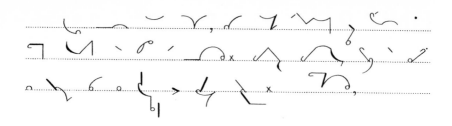

CHALLENGE LETTER

UNIT 2

VOCABULARY BUILDER

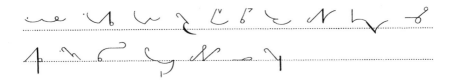

Key

announcement affords fortunate approval china choice final widely automobile accessories roadside appropriate selection furnishings western coast provide

SPECIAL OUTLINES

accept .... except ....

accept means to receive, to agree to.
except means to exclude, to omit, but.

> We *accept* this decision and shall enforce it.
> Everyone was permitted to leave *except* James.

TRANSCRIPTION POINTER

Division of words: To maintain good margins and an attractive appearance in typewritten work, it is sometimes necessary to divide words at the end of a line. Follow these simple rules for word division:

1. Divide words between syllables only.
2. Never divide a one-syllable word, e.g., *freight, stand.*
3. Never divide short words or abbreviations.
4. Never divide before a single-letter syllable, e.g., *defi-nite* NOT *def-inite.*
5. Never separate a one-letter syllable at the beginning or end of a word, e.g., *about* NOT *a-bout, many* NOT *man-y.* Even two-letter syllables should be avoided.
6. Never divide the last word on a page.

5

7. Never divide a hyphenated word except at the hyphen, e.g., *self-control*.

It is not good form to divide words at the end of several lines in succession.

ALWAYS USE A DICTIONARY WHEN IN DOUBT!

1

Crescent .... we consider .... outstanding ....

linens .... Services Department .... preferences ....

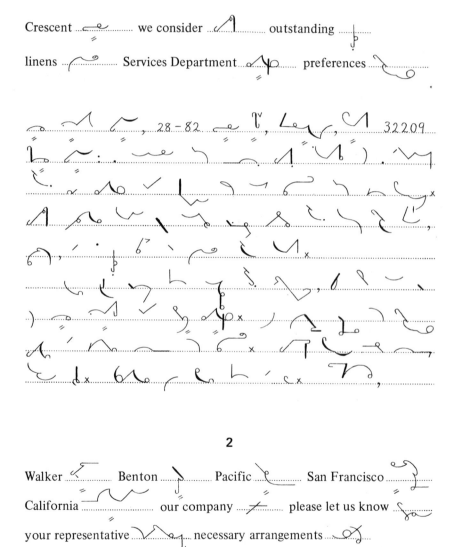

2

Walker .... Benton .... Pacific .... San Francisco ....

California .... our company .... please let us know ....

your representative .... necessary arrangements ....

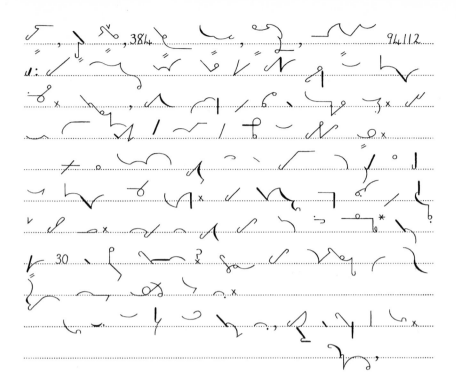

, 384, 94112

* What is an account executive?

3

Los Angeles   specialists   bulletin   ,

sketches   outdoor   wrappers

, 950   , , 90047

7

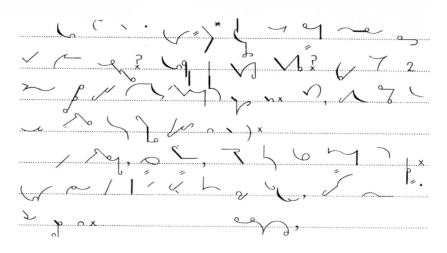

* Why is "full-page" hyphenated?

CHALLENGE LETTER

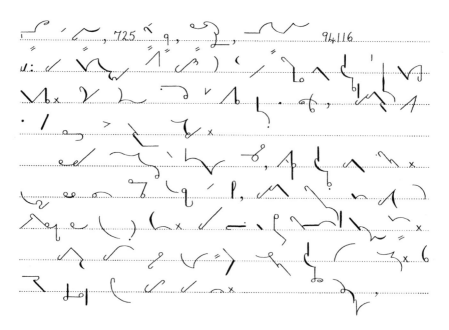

UNIT 3

VOCABULARY BUILDER

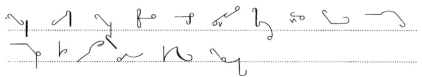

Key

approved wider profitable statistics accident highways drivers clients application campaign capacity talent relations certain television presentation

SPECIAL OUTLINES

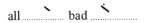

all .... bad ....

For fast transcribing insert the vowel in *bad.* Although the half-length *b* is longer than the symbol for *all,* they could, in fast writing, look somewhat alike.

TRANSCRIPTION POINTER

The comma is placed between the city and state in an address. For example:

New York, New York 10017

There is no space after a comma in typing numbers. For example:

5,000

Never leave a space *before* a comma.

1

Matthews .... Lawton .... Fresno .... equipped ....

legislative .... mutually .... such as ....

Research Departments .... distribution ....

........., 8002 .... 9, ... , ... 93714

J: ....

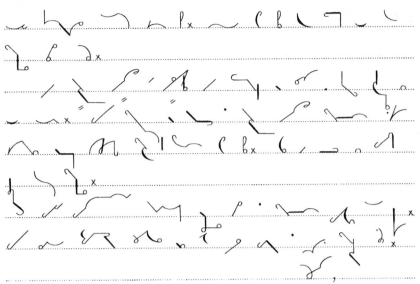

2

Safety ⌇ Sacramento ⌇ majority ⌇

network ⌇

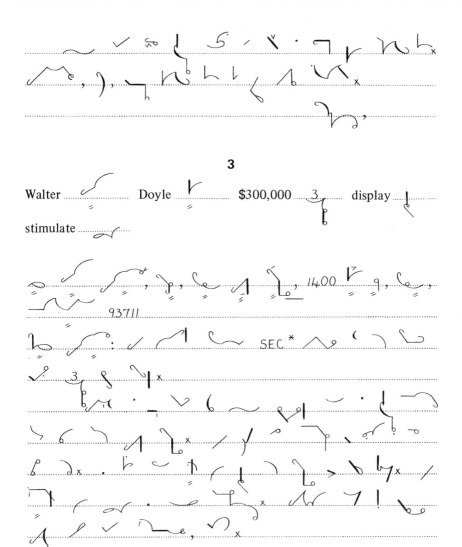

3

Walter   Doyle $300,000   3   display

stimulate

93711

SEC *

* The abbreviation SEC stands for Security Exchange Commission.
The function of the SEC is to regulate stock market activities.

CHALLENGE LETTER

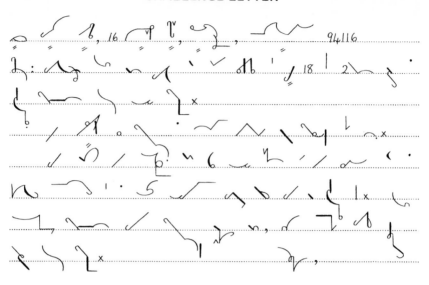

UNIT 4

VOCABULARY BUILDER

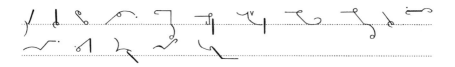

Key

agency decision supplies resuming courtesies extended notified
explanation expires possession agreement marketing ahead assemble
modern fabric

SPECIAL OUTLINES

die, dye

die means to cease to live. It also means a tool used to shape or impress a job.

  dye means to change the color of or stain.
        The man may *die* if the medicine does not arrive in time.
        The *die* was made by the engraver for the printing job.
        We should *dye* this dress because it is faded.

TRANSCRIPTION POINTER

  Two spaces are left after a period, a question mark, or an exclamation point at the end of a sentence.

  It is important to remember that only one space is left after a period in an abbreviation: Dr. Brown.

  In some abbreviations, no space is left: c.o.d., a.m.

  When the period is used as a decimal point, no spacing occurs before or after it: $250.96.

  End of sentence punctuation should always be written in your notes when you take dictation.

Orlando 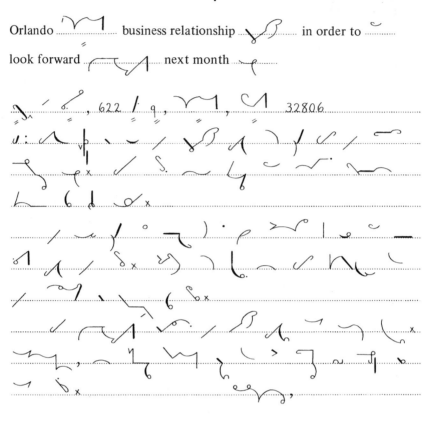 business relationship .... in order to ....

look forward .... next month ....

extended .... terminate .... Production Department ....

* Type the day of the month as a word when the name of the month does not precede it or when it is used alone.

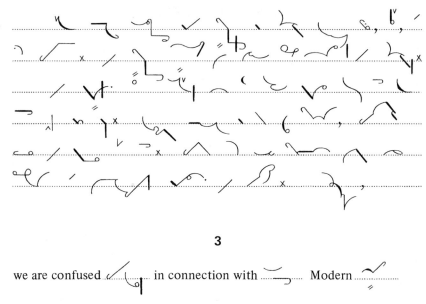

3

we are confused in connection with Modern

* Note that the period is typed before the closing quotation marks.

CHALLENGE LETTER

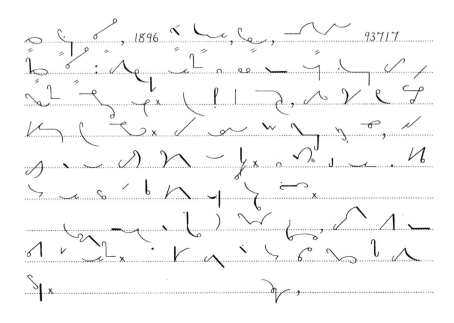

, 1896   93717

UNIT 5

VOCABULARY BUILDER

Key

originally model attempting ideas delighted fine desirable advisable covers preparing refer radio

SPECIAL OUTLINES

accounted ....⌐|.......   amounted ....⌐|....

He *accounted* for the loss by pointing out that no sales were made between July and September.

The bill *amounted* to $385 and we thought it was excessive.

TRANSCRIPTION POINTER

The words *enclosed* and *inclosed* are interchangeable, although *enclosed* is the preferred form. It is important to be consistent in your spelling with each repetition in the letters you write.

If something is to be enclosed in a letter, indicate this by writing the abbreviation *Enc.* or *Inc.* under the initials at the end of the letter. The enclosure is not noted on the envelope.

There are many acceptable ways of indicating the initials and the enclosures in business letters. Here are some:

DI:YO	DI:YO	DI:yo	DI/YO
ENC.	Enc.	enc.	ENC.

1

Weber 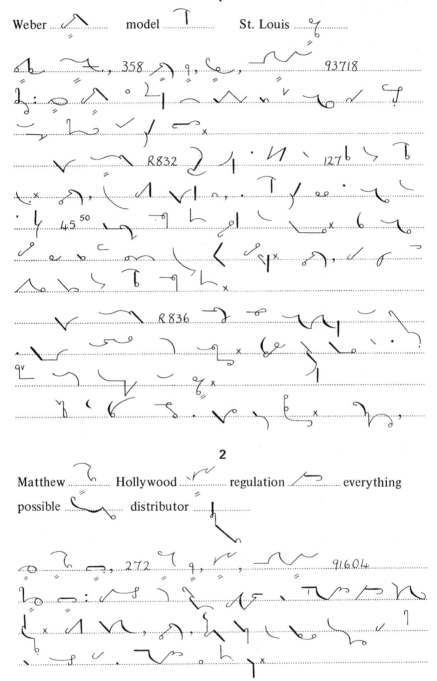 model St. Louis

358 93718

R832 127 45 50

R836

2

Matthew Hollywood regulation everything

possible distributor

272 91604

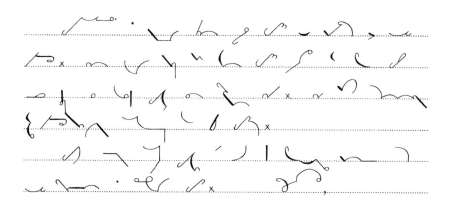

3

Carmel 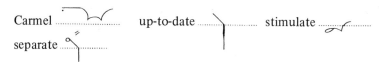 up-to-date stimulate

separate

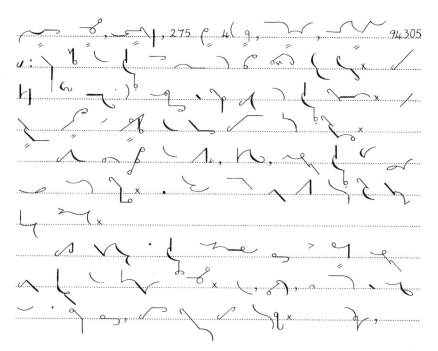

CHALLENGE LETTER

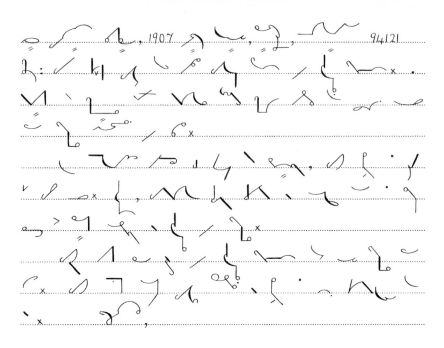

2 Printing and Publishing

UNIT 1

VOCABULARY BUILDER

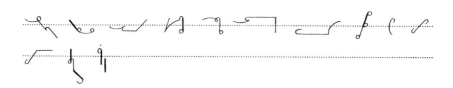

Key

newspaper business inquiry children's mysteries incorrect quickly suggestions through win week distribution considered

SPECIAL OUTLINES

past   passed

past (adjective) of or relating to time gone by; out of the reach of.
passed (verb) gone, moved, proceeded.

You have been notified in the *past* of these events.

The parade *passed* by our door.

TRANSCRIPTION POINTER

Commas are used to set off parenthetical words that could be omitted from the sentence. For example:

I shall be ready, of course, when you are.

We shall, therefore, submit our responses on the same day.

21

1

Powell 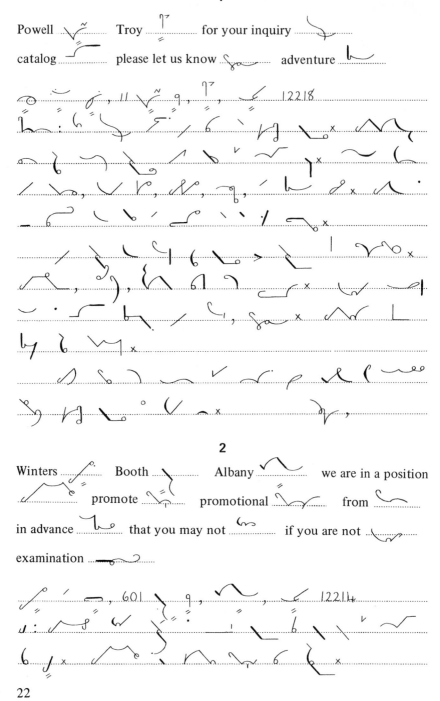 Troy for your inquiry

catalog please let us know adventure

2

Winters Booth Albany we are in a position

promote promotional from

in advance that you may not if you are not

examination

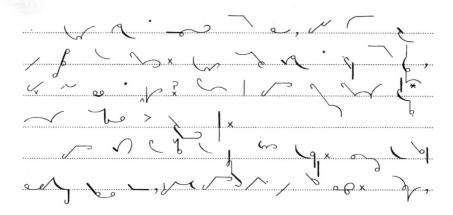

* What is meant by promotional advertising?

3

Beacon ....\............ Rochester ....⌀......... we are very sorry ..../.........

impossible ....⌒......... we are anxious ..../.......... friendship ......𝒮.........

within the next ......⋀........⌐........

23

CHALLENGE LETTER

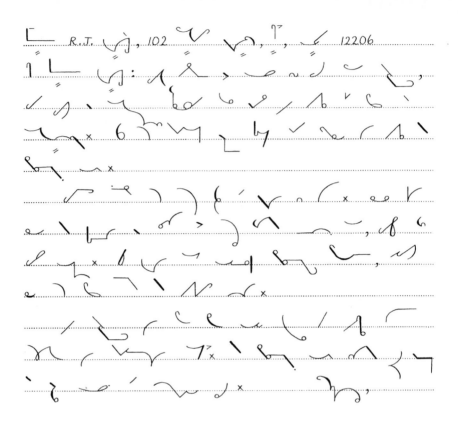

UNIT 2

VOCABULARY BUILDER

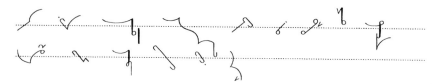

Key

really completely introduced informative reprint heating serious ideas incidentally fuels proud industry printer printing easier

SPECIAL OUTLINES

special-ly .... especial-ly ....

Messrs. .... (abbreviated from the French *Messieurs* and used for

the plural of *mister*).

Messrs. Brown, Stover, and Blake are coming to the meeting.

TRANSCRIPTION POINTER

Commas are used to set off words in direct address. For example:
We believe, Mr. Wilson, that you should accept the position.
We do not agree with you, Mr. President, that he is inexperienced.

Compare:

We believe that Mr. Jones should be present at the meeting.

1

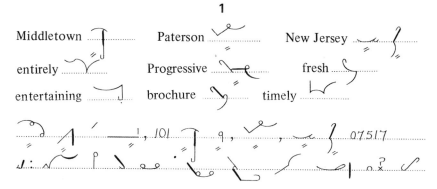

Middletown .... Paterson .... New Jersey ....

entirely .... Progressive .... fresh ....

entertaining .... brochure .... timely ....

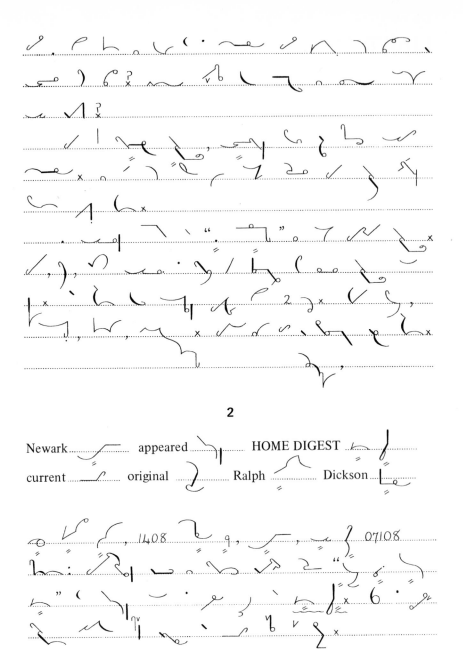

2

Newark......_____ appeared ......_____ HOME DIGEST ......_____

current ......_____ original ......_____ Ralph ......_____ Dickson ......_____

* What is a reprint fee?

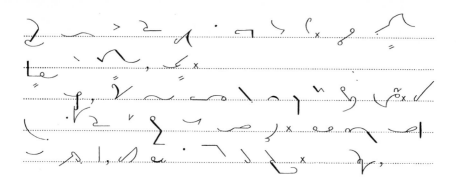

3

Jersey City ⸱⸱⸱⸱⸱⸱⸱⸱⸱⸱ forthcoming ⸱⸱⸱⸱⸱⸱⸱⸱⸱⸱ in which we think

you will be ⸱⸱⸱⸱⸱⸱⸱⸱⸱⸱ frank ⸱⸱⸱⸱⸱⸱⸱⸱⸱⸱ personal ⸱⸱⸱⸱⸱⸱⸱⸱⸱⸱ any business

⸱⸱⸱⸱⸱⸱⸱⸱⸱⸱ any company ⸱⸱⸱⸱⸱⸱⸱⸱⸱⸱ for this reason ⸱⸱⸱⸱⸱⸱⸱⸱⸱⸱

UNIT 3

VOCABULARY BUILDER

Key

renew teacher's music education pupils chief variation include similar inks field meeting either radio

SPECIAL OUTLINES

special-ly ⟨outline⟩ ⟨outline⟩ specialize ⟨outline⟩ specialty ⟨outline⟩ specialist ⟨outline⟩

At college, you should *specialize* in music.
His *specialty* is card tricks.
He is a *specialist* in tax accounting.

TRANSCRIPTION POINTER

Salutations in common usage include:

Dear Sir	My dear Sir
Dear Mr. Grant	My dear Mr. Crosby
Dear Miss Murphy	My dear Madam

When *Dear* is the first word in the salutation, it is capitalized.
When *My* precedes *dear,* a small *d* is used for the adjective.

1

Bridgeport ⟨outline⟩ Connecticut ⟨outline⟩ specialty ⟨outline⟩

high schools ⟨outline⟩ chief concerns ⟨outline⟩

29

06606

2

Fowler　　　Regent　　　New Haven

Atlantic　　　combined　　　edition　　　technical

tremendous

06518

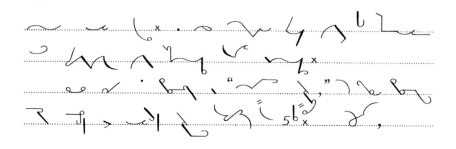

3

at once  estimating ⟩ offset ⌐⟍ guarantee ⟍⌐

wealth ⟋⟍ enclosed ⟍⌐ card ⟍⌐

---

* Why is *money-back* hyphenated?

CHALLENGE LETTER

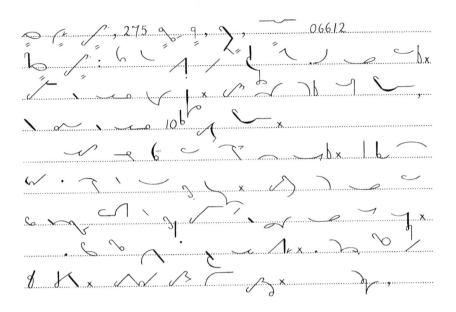

UNIT 4

VOCABULARY BUILDER

Key

continue through weekly community eager fiction inspiring convince county experiences humor

SPECIAL OUTLINES

county ⌐ country ⟋ community ⌐

A *county* is a large division for local government.

A *country* is the territory of a nation.

A *community* is a region or the people of a particular region.

There are twelve *counties* in this state.

You should not compare what happens in a foreign *country* with our national policies.

As a good member of your *community,* you should help your neighbors in times of distress.

TRANSCRIPTION POINTER

Words or phrases in a series are separated by commas. The comma before the conjunction may either be omitted or inserted.

For example:

We are selling hats, coats, shoes, and accessories.

Will you eat peas, lamb and salad?

We enjoyed ourselves walking in the country, skiing on the slopes, or riding through the forest.

1

Deal ⌐ gardening ⌐ so many people ⌐

their own ⌐ column ⌐

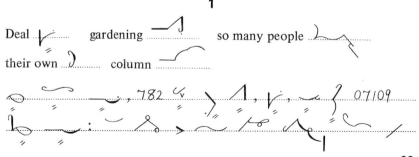

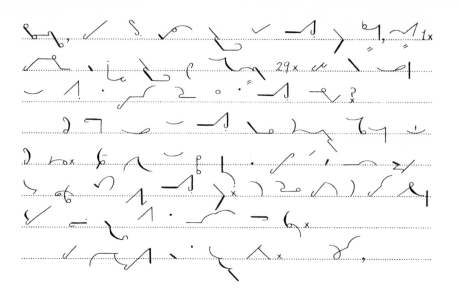

2

Red Bank ⟨shorthand⟩ Newell ⟨shorthand⟩ aroused ⟨shorthand⟩ editors ⟨shorthand⟩

in accordance with ⟨shorthand⟩ anticipate ⟨shorthand⟩

3

Philip 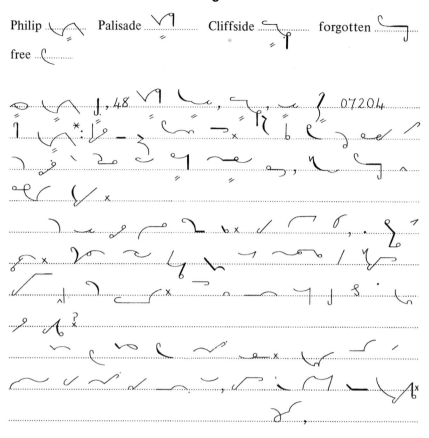 Palisade Cliffside forgotten

free

* Business men frequently use first names when writing business letters to people with whom they are friendly.

CHALLENGE LETTER

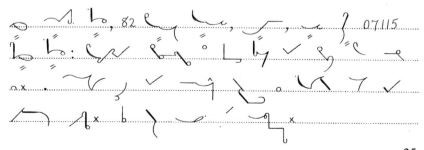

35

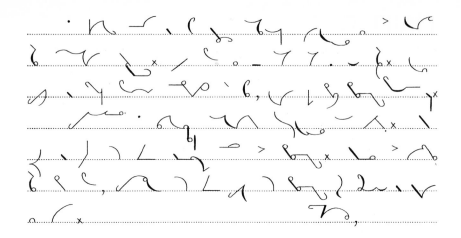

UNIT 5

VOCABULARY BUILDER

Key

superior suitable appropriately gift loose even finished instruct imprinted winter

SPECIAL OUTLINES

lose ...⟋⟍...... loose ...⟋⟍......

lose means to be parted from, to be unsuccessful.
loose means free, not attached.

> Did you *lose* your watch?
> I prefer to wear clothing which is *loose* fitting.

TRANSCRIPTION POINTER

The first line of the inside address of a letter is the clue to the salutation. These two must always be in agreement.

Items such as "Personal" or "Room No." are typed two spaces below the return address in the top, left-hand corner of the envelope.

1

Plastic .....⟋..... Philadelphia.....⟍..... Pennsylvania .....⟍⟋.....

adhere .....⟍⟋..... background .....⟍⟋..... designer .....⟍.....

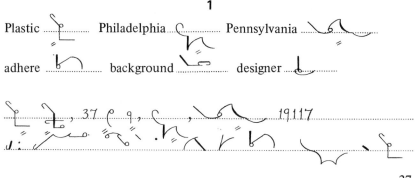

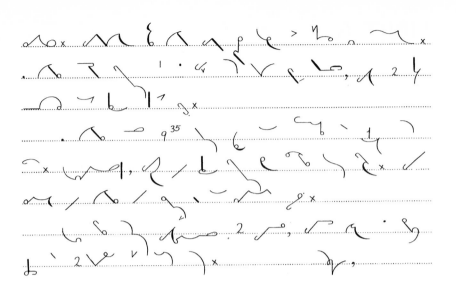

2

Bergen 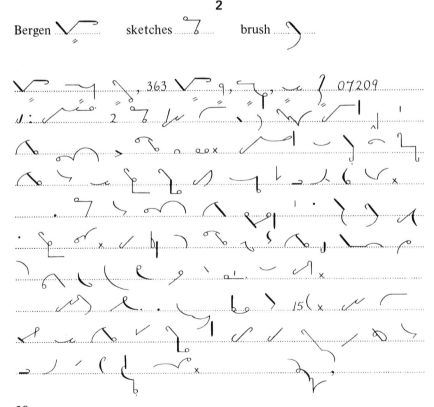 sketches brush

38

as soon as .... ahead .... undoubtedly ....

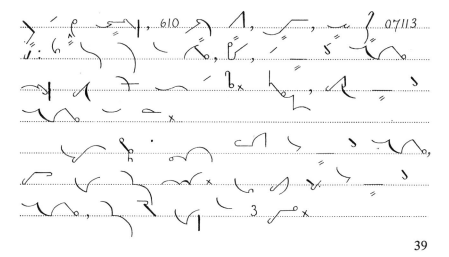

* A dependent clause should be followed by a comma.

CHALLENGE LETTER

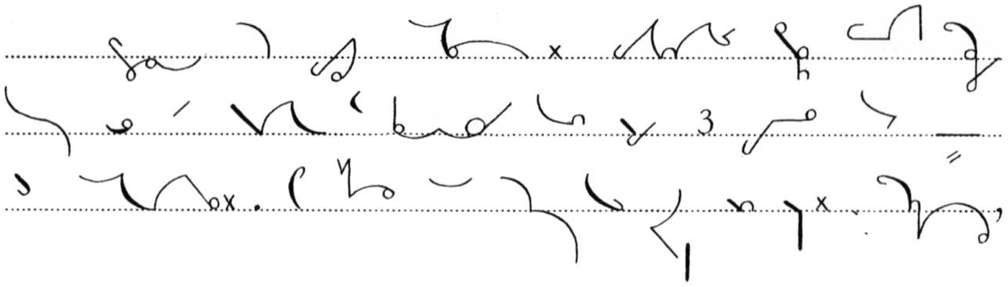

3

Basic Industries

UNIT 1

VOCABULARY BUILDER

Key

raising situation conditions oils considerably maintenance constantly outlines satisfied basement service

SPECIAL OUTLINES

advise, advice

advise (*verb*). It means to recommend a course of action, to counsel.
advice (*noun*). It means a recommendation for a course of action.

    I shall *advise* the committee on nominations.
    We know you value his *advice* and shall follow it.

TRANSCRIPTION POINTER

An appositive (a word or group of words following the noun and giving information about it) is set off by commas:

    John, the janitor, fixed the door.
    Mary, her friend from camp, has not arrived.

1

Farmingdale 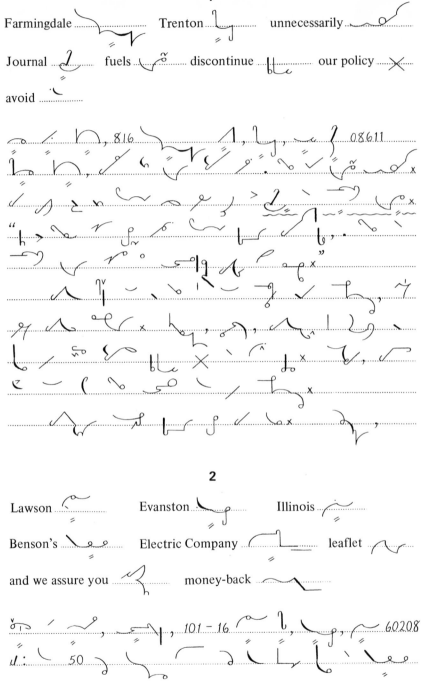 Trenton unnecessarily

Journal fuels discontinue our policy

avoid

Lawson Evanston Illinois

Benson's Electric Company leaflet

and we assure you money-back

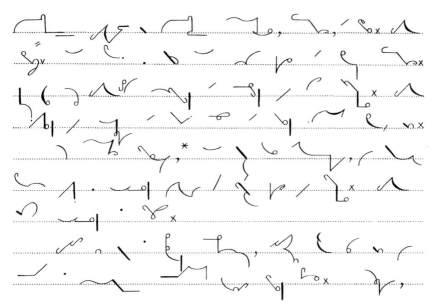

* What is the meaning of *personnel*?

3

Ralston ⁓⁓⁓ Lawyers ⁓⁓⁓ Smedley ⁓⁓⁓ area ⁓⁓⁓

outlets ⁓⁓⁓ wires ⁓⁓⁓ determining ⁓⁓⁓

at one time ⁓⁓⁓

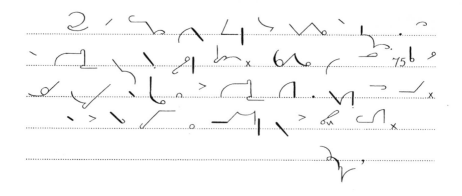

CHALLENGE LETTER

UNIT 2

VOCABULARY BUILDER

Key

discuss plates advance sincerely plastic includes size exact system experience spiral elevators

SPECIAL OUTLINES

assistance ....⌐.....   assistants ....⌐....

assistance is help.

assistants are the people giving the help.

We had three *assistants* to help us, and their *assistance* was most valuable.

TRANSCRIPTION POINTER

Words like *well, yes, no, why* etc., are followed by commas when used at the beginning of a sentence. For example:

Yes, we received your check.

Well, we were certainly surprised.

No, it is not too late.

1

Warde ....   modernization ....   competitive ....
competitors ....   schedule ....   that this arrangement ....
stimulate ....

W.H. .... , 62 .... 9, ... 07114 ....

....

....

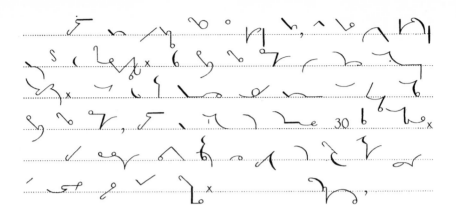

2

acetate _____ nylon _____ inventory _____ sheets _____

pattern _____ any inquiries _____ workmanship _____

immediate attention _____

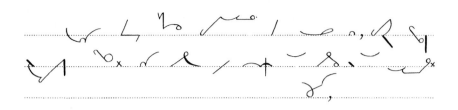

3

Hardware .... this will confirm .... wire ....

exactly .... as soon as we receive .... vitally ....

B. ...., 101 - 16 ...., ... 07517

.... * ....

.... , 39 , 62 , 69 x ....

....

....

....

2 ....

....

....

....

* What is the meaning of *spiral*?

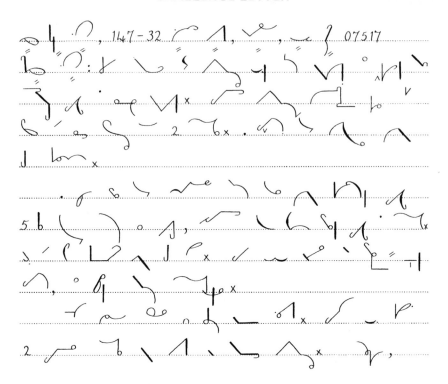

UNIT 3

VOCABULARY BUILDER

Key

salary negotiations points summary sound articles president districts displayed

SPECIAL OUTLINES

correspondence .... correspondents ....

To *correspond* is to write or exchange letters. The letters in the exchange are the *correspondence*. The people who correspond are the *correspondents*.

We received your folder of *correspondence* on the subject.

The two *correspondents* wrote to each other daily.

TRANSCRIPTION POINTER

Items in dates are separated by commas, as in:

On December 7, 1941, Pearl Harbor was attacked.

Today is Friday, June 12.

1

Parson .... Royal .... to make arrangements ....

workers .... union .... local .... management ....

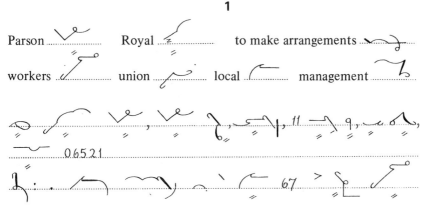

49

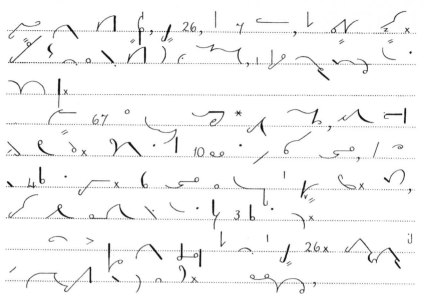

* Can you define *negotiations*?

2

Wilder 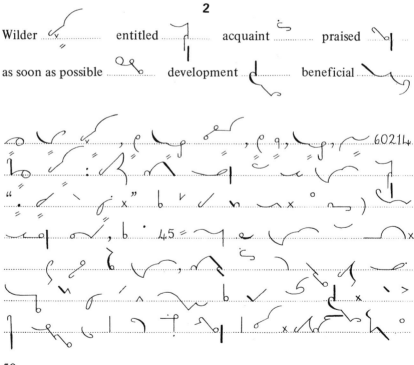   entitled   acquaint   praised

as soon as possible   development   beneficial

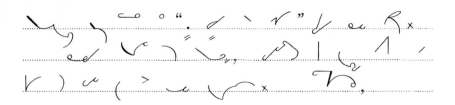

3

merchandising 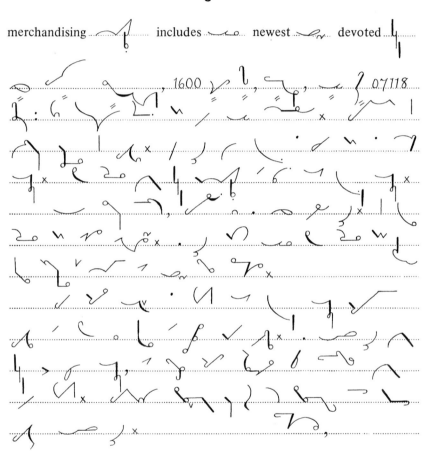 includes ⌒⌒ newest ⌒ devoted ⌐

CHALLENGE LETTER

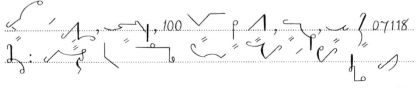

UNIT 4

VOCABULARY BUILDER

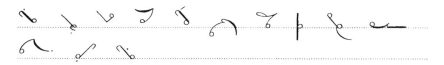

Key

brass position parts anxious bronze silver stainless decide specify single solving concern praise

SPECIAL OUTLINES

simple ....⌒.... sample ....⌒.... example ....⌒....

In addition to writing the outline correctly and in the proper position, think of the sense of the sentence in determining whether the word is *simple* or *sample*:

It was *simple* to repair the bicycle.

I have a *sample* of the fabric.

TRANSCRIPTION POINTER

Numbers under ten should be written in words:

six cases	six dollars
20 pints	$20

In writing amounts of money, use the decimal for cents:

$20.60

Omit the decimal when writing dollars alone:

$20

1

trade ....⌐.... we hope that you are in a position ....⌒....

particularly ....⌒.... copper ....⌒.... nickel ....⌒....

engineering department ....⌒.... your response ....⌒....

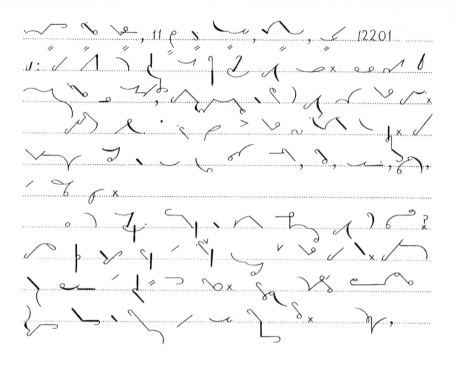

2

Philadelphia 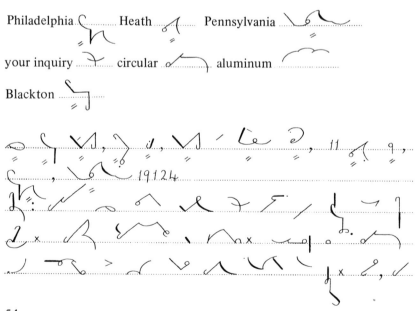 Heath Pennsylvania

your inquiry circular aluminum

Blackton

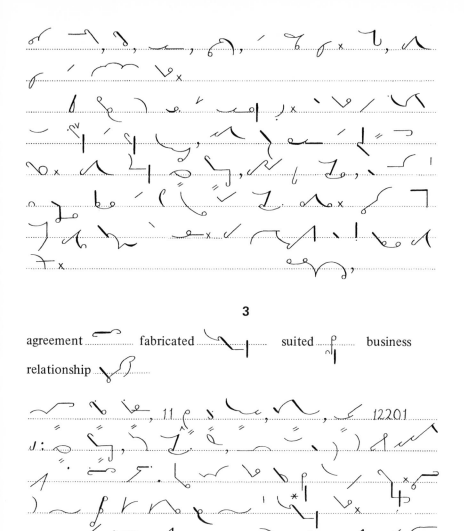

3

agreement ⁓ fabricated ⁓ suited ⁓ business

relationship ⁓

* What is the meaning of *fabricated* and *prefabricated*?

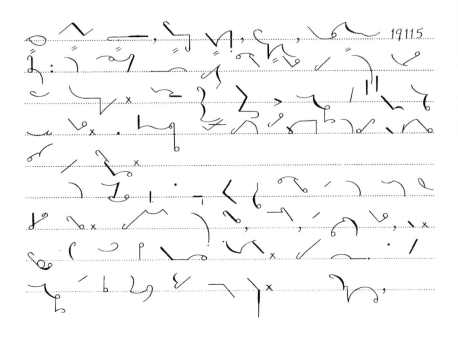

UNIT 5

VOCABULARY BUILDER

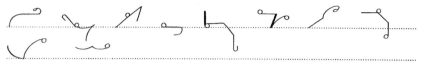

Key

locations personnel research section descriptive schedules relations acceptance folders announce

SPECIAL OUTLINES

Mrs. or Misses

Mrs. is the title used for a married woman.

Misses is the title used for several unmarried girls.

I knew *Mrs.* Rosen before she married.

The *Misses* Clark and Webster are the nurses on duty.

TRANSCRIPTION POINTER

Typewritten work must be proofread before it is removed from the typewriter. The job does not end with the typing of it — each page should be proofread as it is completed. When you proofread, examine the copy for typing errors which you were unaware of as you worked. Also, compare your finished copy with your working copy or shorthand notes to be sure that you have not omitted or changed anything.

If you find errors, the corrections should be made on the carbon copies also so that you have corrected copies for interoffice distribution and for your files.

1

Houston   Saunders   quickly   wealth

updated   printed

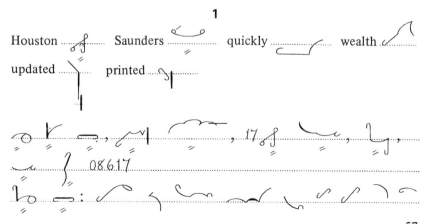

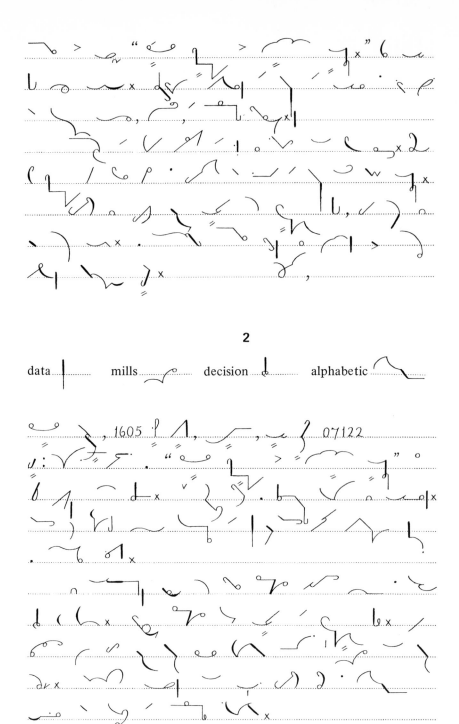

2

data | mills decision alphabetic

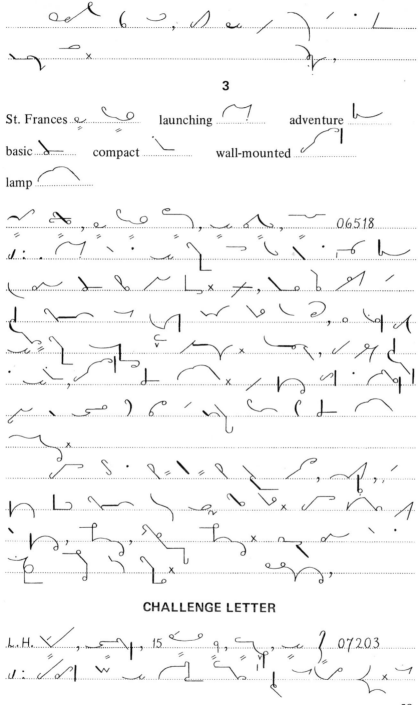

3

St. Frances .... launching .... adventure

basic .... compact .... wall-mounted ....

lamp ....

.... 0.6518

CHALLENGE LETTER

L.H. .... , 15 .... , ... 0.7203

Fashion

UNIT 1

VOCABULARY BUILDER

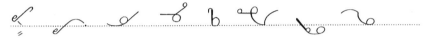

Key

Swan swimming necessary accessories dresses successful businesses emphasis

TRANSCRIPTION POINTER

When typing the titles of books, all words in the title should be capitalized *except* conjunctions, prepositions, and articles:

I have just read "Gone with the Wind."

When typing the titles of magazines and newspapers current styling books recommend that the article *the* be omitted even though it appears on the cover, title page, or masthead of the publication:

I read it in the "New York Times."

When titles are typed in uppercase letters, all the words should be capitalized:

Do you subscribe to the JOURNAL OF COMMERCE?

1

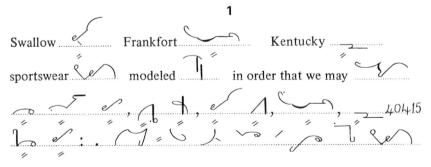

Swallow .... Frankfort .... Kentucky ....

sportswear .... modeled .... in order that we may ....

.... 404 15

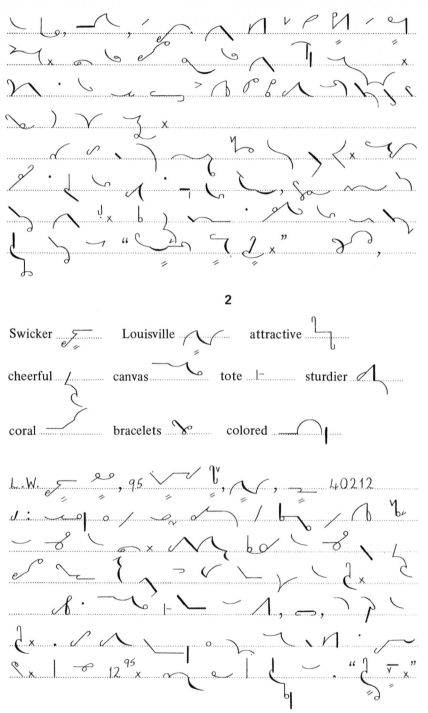

2

Swicker .... Louisville .... attractive ....

cheerful .... canvas .... tote .... sturdier ....

coral .... bracelets .... colored ....

L.W. .... , 95 .... , ... , ... 40212

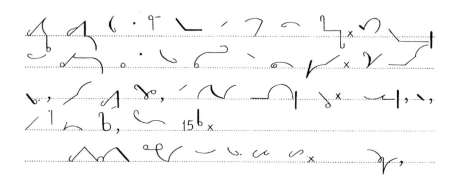

3

Santa Fe New Mexico importing

exporting creating tariff drastic

draft findings

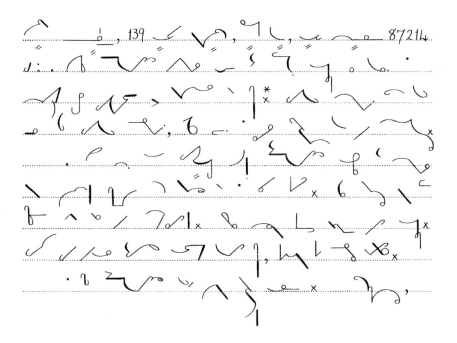

---

* What is meant by the *balance of trade*?

CHALLENGE LETTER

UNIT 2

VOCABULARY BUILDER

Key

chances basis impresses promises causes swatch

SPECIAL OUTLINES

convenience (*noun*) meaning suitable, comfort giving, fit.
convince (*verb*) meaning to prove or satisfy by proof.

The taxi service was a great *convenience* and we reached the theater without rushing.

We shall *convince* you of the importance of being on time.

TRANSCRIPTION POINTER

Trade names, brand names, and commercial products are capitalized.

The common noun which follows the name of the product is capitalized only when it is used as part of the firm name:

General Electric Radios
television sets and radios

1

fabrics .... refinished .... adjustments ....

assume the .... shrinkage ....

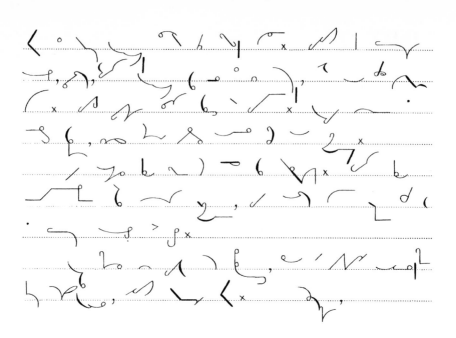

2

Platt 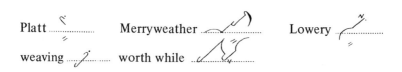 Merryweather .... Lowery ....

weaving .... worth while ....

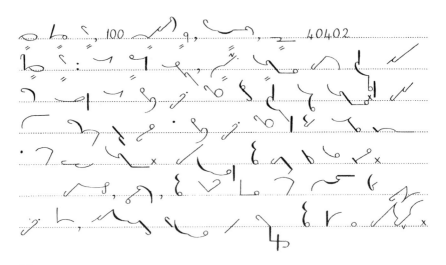

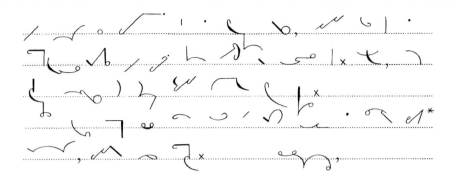

* What is a *swatch*?

3

Empire 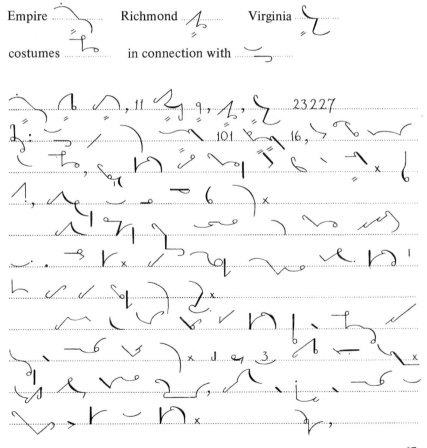 Richmond Virginia

costumes in connection with

* * *

CHALLENGE LETTER

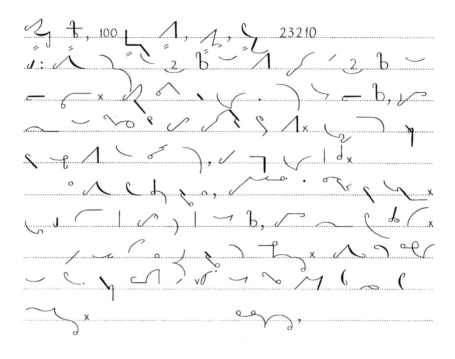

UNIT 3

VOCABULARY BUILDER

Key

sweater allowances courses classes responses

SPECIAL OUTLINES

addition ᒍ   edition ᒍ

An *addition* is something that has been added; an increase.

An *edition* is a published form of a literary work.

>We appreciated the *addition* of three nurses to the staff.

>When can we expect the third *edition* of this book?

TRANSCRIPTION POINTER

When writing an address as part of the body of a letter, it is not necessary to arrange it in separate lines as you do on an envelope. Instead, it may be written in sentence form, with each part followed by a comma:

>I may be addressed at 276 Broad Street, New Haven, Connecticut 06417.

>You may send the package to Mrs. Clara Hobson, 77–48 Southern Boulevard, Topeka, Kansas 66610.

1

Drummer ⸝ Medlock ⸝ Norfolk ⸝ Knitwear ⸝

which have been ⸝ in business ⸝ chain ⸝ stitch ⸝

for many years ⸝ competitive ⸝

⸝ ⸝, 11 ⸝ 9, ⸝, ⸝ 23505

⸝ ⸝ ⸝, ⸝ ⸝ ⸝ x ⸝

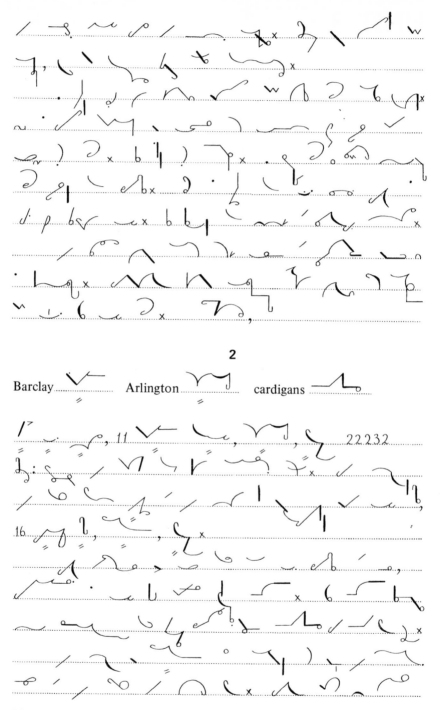

2

Barclay ⌄‾ Arlington ⌄⌐ cardigans ⌐⌐

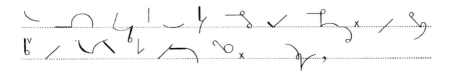

3

Alexandria  Institute  lectures

consumer adapted determine

comprehensive

* Fashion and style differ in meaning to the extent that style never changes but fashion does. Fashion is the style being used at a specific time.

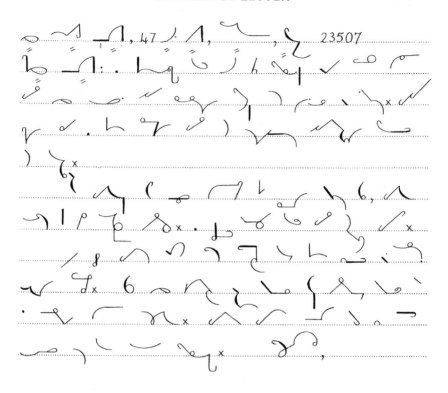

UNIT 4

VOCABULARY BUILDER

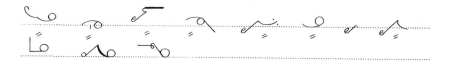

Key

Francis Moses Swagger Mississippi Sweeney United States suite
Swift taxes services expresses

SPECIAL OUTLINES

either (or)....(........ neither (nor)...........

(Note that *either* is followed by *or* and *neither* is followed by *nor*.)

Use *either* red or yellow paint on the terrace floor.

We found *neither* the long nor the short pair of slacks.

TRANSCRIPTION POINTER

Nonrestrictive (not necessary to the sentence) phrases are set off by commas.

Restrictive (necessary to the sentence) phrases are not set off by commas. For example:

1. Nonrestrictive phrase:

John, who was standing near the door, called to us as we entered.

2. Restrictive phrase:

The boy who was standing near the door called to us as we entered.

1

frequently .... newcomer .... mathematics ....

beginners .... graduates .... interview ....

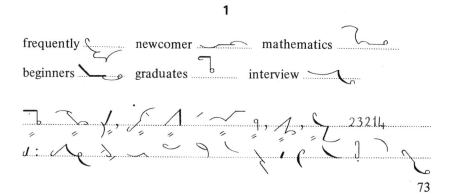

2

comparison ⌇ we think you will agree that the ⌇

compared ⌇ yarn ⌇ unhappy ⌇

(shorthand text) , 14 , 9 , 235.13

* How does a comparison shopper get information about competitive products?

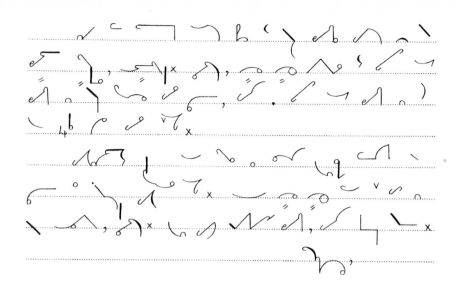

3

Cantor ⌐ area ⟩ scheduled ⁊ join ⟋

Jewel ⟋ territory ⋁⋁

87.216

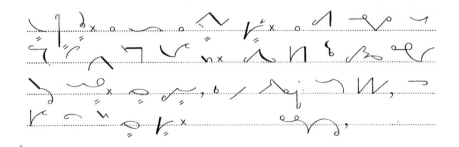

CHALLENGE LETTER

UNIT 5

VOCABULARY BUILDER

Key

Swicker   foxes   commences   sizes

SPECIAL OUTLINES

fewer .... less ....

Fewer refers to number. *Less* refers to quantity.

There are *fewer* packages in the book case than on the floor.

There is *less* fat in this brand of margarine.

TRANSCRIPTION POINTER

Use commas to separate main clauses joined by *and, but, or, nor,* and
yet, unless clauses are very short:

1. Main clauses:

In the morning we fed the chickens, and the farmer took care of all the
other chores.

There are a few islands in these waters, but there are thousands of islands
in the Pacific Ocean.

2. No commas:

I will go and I will not wait.

We went to Washington and saw the Capitol and the White House.

1

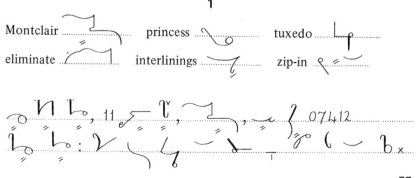

Montclair .... princess .... tuxedo ....

eliminate .... interlinings .... zip-in ....

2

Ashland 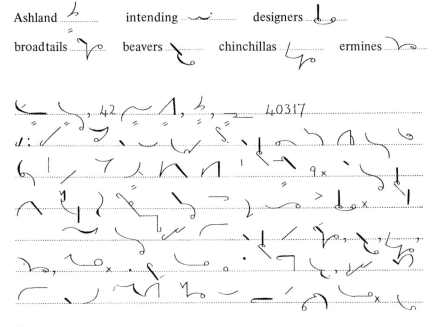 intending   designers

broadtails beavers   chinchillas   ermines

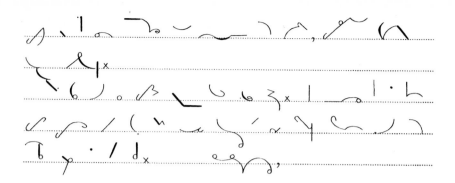

3

Hoboken .... semi-annual .... anklets .... tropical ....
broadcloth .... oxford .... millinery department ....

5 Apology, Complaint, Adjustment, Appreciation

UNIT 1

VOCABULARY BUILDER

Key

Lester Cloister replaced dismissed stored enclosed best trust

TRANSCRIPTION POINTER

The line space release should be used at the end of a line to keep the right margin as uniform as possible.

Divide a word between syllables if you cannot complete it. However, try not to have too many successive lines ending with a syllabicated word.

1

Rhonda ⌒ Phoenix ⌒ Arizona ⌒ sidewalk ⌒

inspector ⌒ complaints ⌒ shattered ⌒ violation ⌒

⌒ 1607 ⌒ 85021

⌒ : ⌒ 16 ⌒

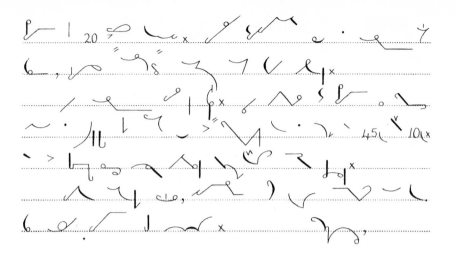

2

last month 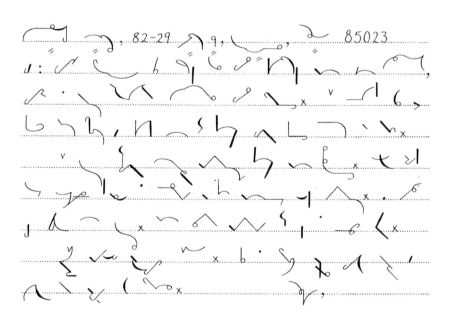 feared insurance company

to do business

3

Melody 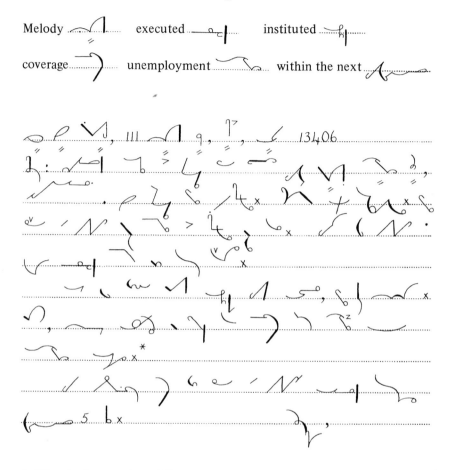 executed _____ instituted _____

coverage _____ unemployment _____ within the next _____

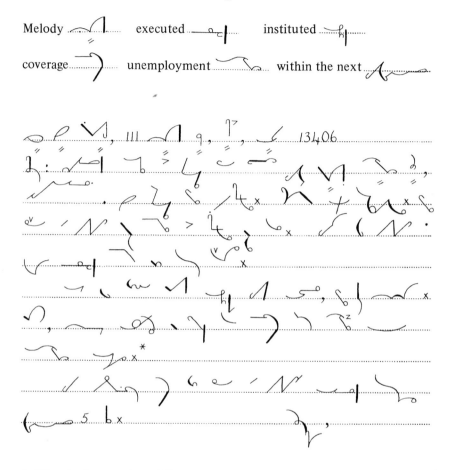

* What is the meaning of "being covered by unemployment insurance"?

CHALLENGE LETTER

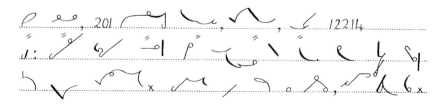

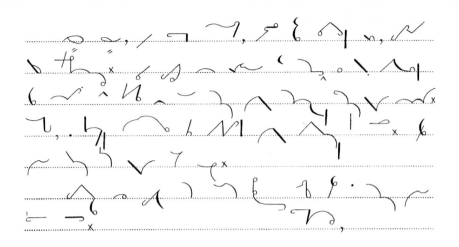

UNIT 2

VOCABULARY BUILDER

Key

last crust raised costs just pressed analyzed noticed promised

SPECIAL OUTLINES

statement ... 𝒍ₒ ..... settlement ... 𝒍ₒ ....

TRANSCRIPTION POINTER

In an inside address the number of the house should be written as a number:

46 Baker Drive (except 1, as in One East 72 Street)

The apartment or room number should also be written as a number:

Room 406

Apartment 11

The name of the street or avenue should be written out only if it is under ten:

45 Fifth Avenue

BUT

27 East 106 Street

The *th*, *nd*, *rd* may be omitted from street names.

1

Tucson .... pastry .... exactly .... completely ....

reputation ....

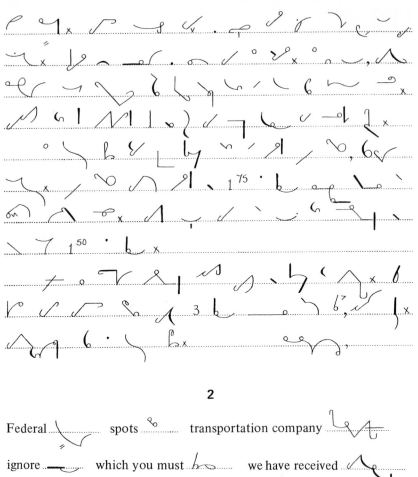

2

Federal ⌇ spots ⌇ transportation company ⌇

ignore ⌇ which you must ⌇ we have received ⌇

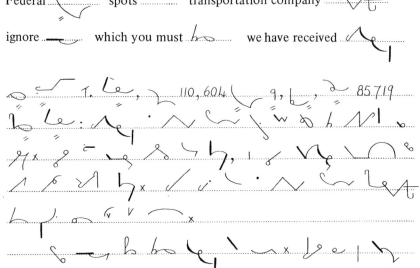

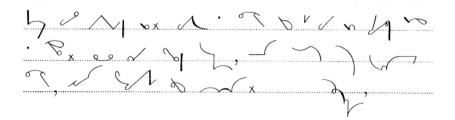

3

Brewster 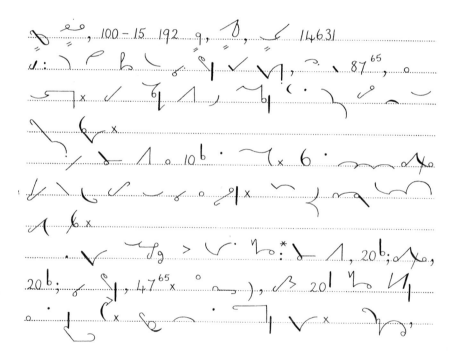 incorrect   service charge

you must be   consists

---

* Note the use of the colon after the words "following items" and before a series of items.

87

CHALLENGE LETTER

UNIT 3

VOCABULARY BUILDER

Key

creased used request against Duster faster rust

SPECIAL OUTLINES

finish-ed

financial-ly

furnish

TRANSCRIPTION POINTER

Use a comma after an introductory clause, phrase, or series of phrases:

As soon as you finish, we will also be ready.
Leaving me to do the work, my friend read a book.
On the evening of the tenth, we went to the movies.

1

Yuma   reconcile   processed

this matter

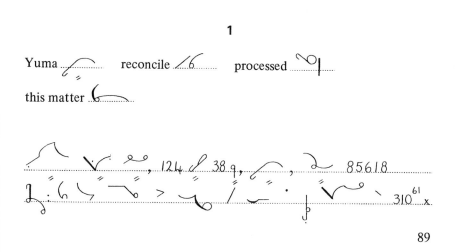

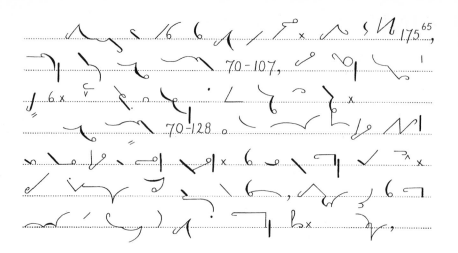

2

debit ⌐..... unfortunately ～⌐ misplaced ～⌐ enable us ～.

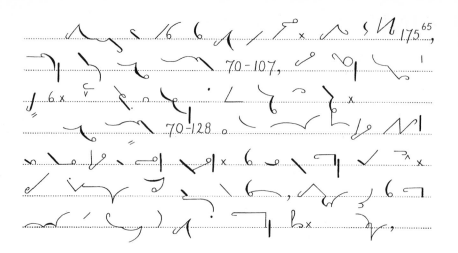

---

* What is a debit?

Honolulu 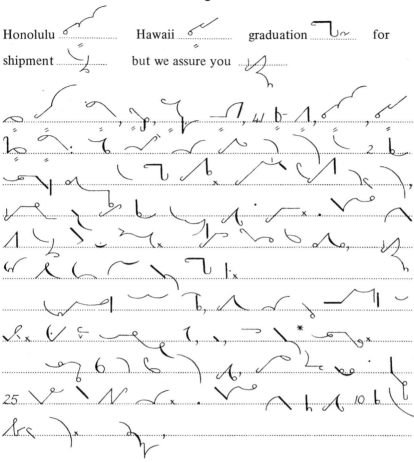 Hawaii graduation for

shipment but we assure you

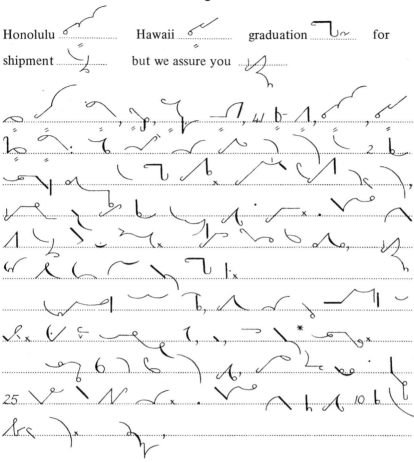

* Note the spelling for *bear* meaning *carry*.

CHALLENGE LETTER

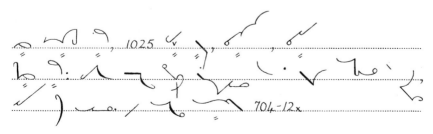

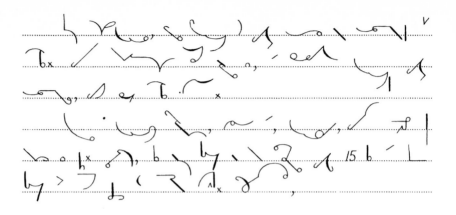

UNIT 4

VOCABULARY BUILDER

Key

Webster upholster style experienced artistic West invest fixed

SPECIAL OUTLINES

next .... newest ....

TRANSCRIPTION POINTER

Use a comma between two separate adjectives:
We saw tall, red flowers.

If one adjective seems to modify the combined final adjective and the noun, there is no comma:
It was an old summer dress.

1

Columbia .... South Carolina ....

furniture .... upholsterers ....

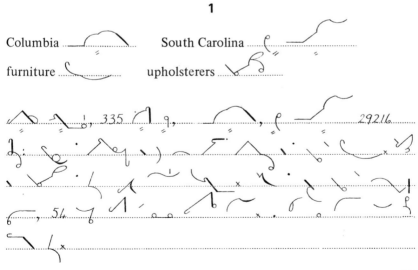

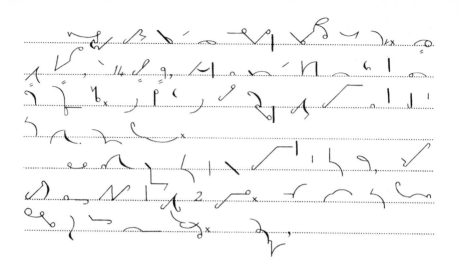

2

Charleston 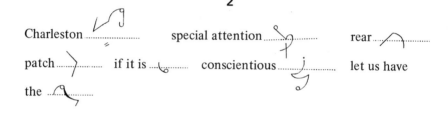 special attention 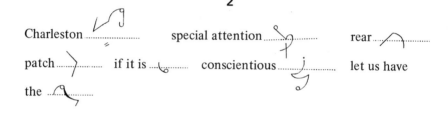 rear

patch if it is conscientious let us have

the

94

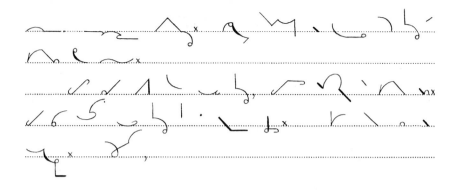

3

Stanford 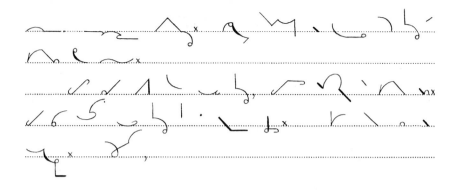 artists assortment next

month

* Note the spelling of *capitol* when referring to the building.

CHALLENGE LETTER

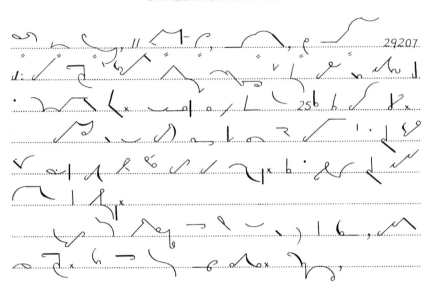

29207.

UNIT 5

VOCABULARY BUILDER

Key
Foster   increased   suggestions   rest

SPECIAL OUTLINES

gladly ....⌒....... greatly ....⟩....... grateful ......⌐.......

TRANSCRIPTION POINTER

Names of school subjects are all written with a small letter except for languages. Course names followed by numbers are capitalized:

We study English, Spanish, history, and typewriting.

I registered for History 110.

1

Real Estate ...⌒....)....... premises ......↘⌀....... current ......⟋.......

approximate ......↘⌀....... tenants ....↓⌀...........

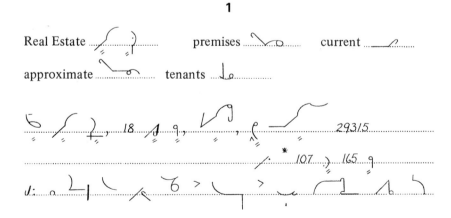

* *RE:* means *in reference to*.

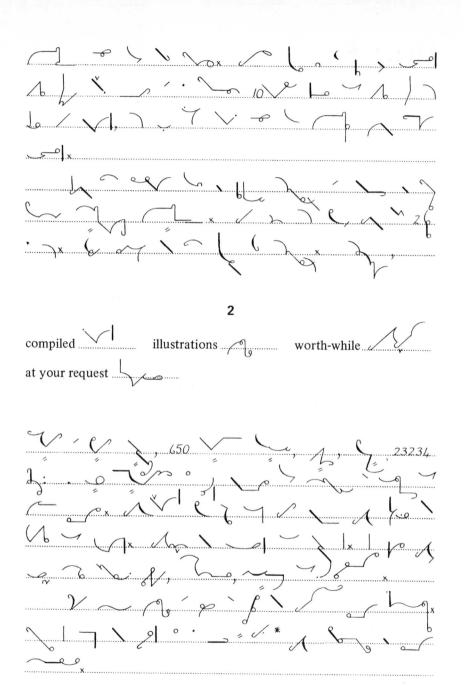

2

compiled .... illustrations .... worth-while ....

at your request ....

* What is a give-away?

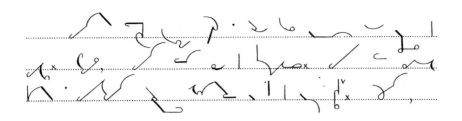

3

Knitwear 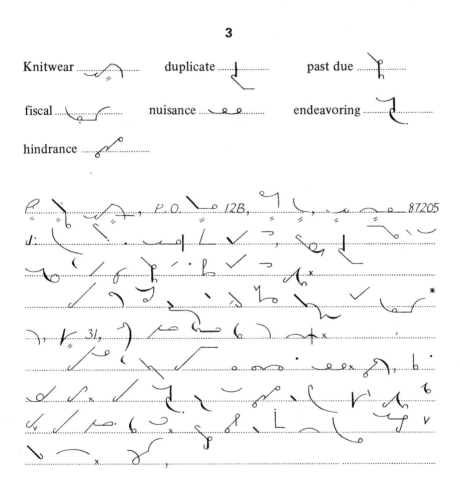 duplicate ⎽⎽⎽ past due ⎽⎽⎽

fiscal ⎽⎽⎽ nuisance ⎽⎽⎽ endeavoring ⎽⎽⎽

hindrance ⎽⎽⎽

P.O. ⎽⎽⎽ 12B, ⎽⎽⎽ 87205

* What is the meaning of *fiscal*?

CHALLENGE LETTER

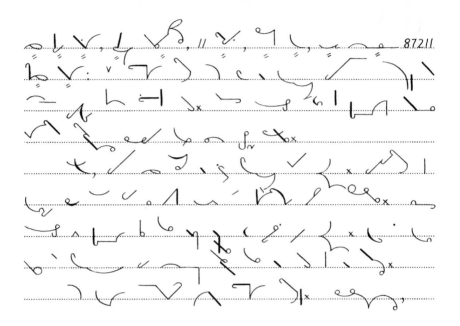

87.2.11.

100

6 Travel and Transportation

UNIT 1

VOCABULARY BUILDER

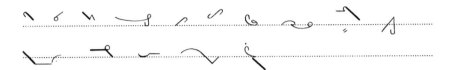

Key

broad hot about understand rent want friends mountains October
written booklet exhibit indicate import comfortable

SPECIAL OUTLINES

latest .... least ....

lowest .... last ....

TRANSCRIPTION POINTER

When a page of notes has been transcribed, a diagonal line drawn across
the page "cancels" the notes.

1

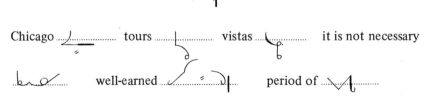

Chicago .... tours .... vistas .... it is not necessary
.... well-earned .... period of ....

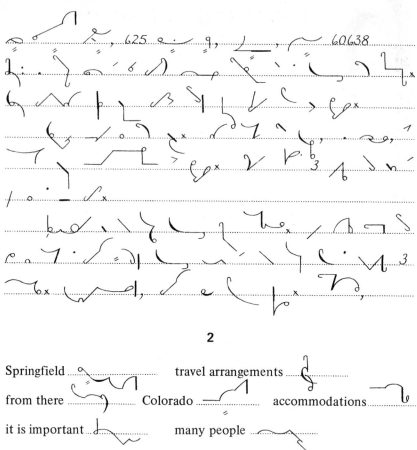

2

Springfield 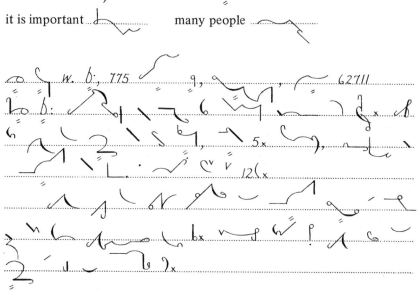 travel arrangements

from there ... Colorado ... accommodations

it is important ... many people ...

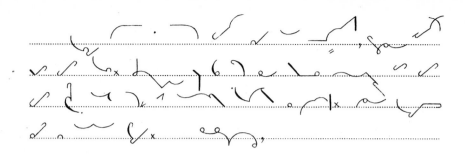

3

Gary 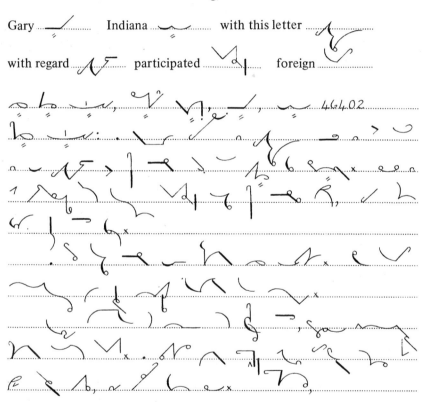 Indiana ‎with this letter‎

with regard ‎participated‎ foreign

46402

CHALLENGE LETTER

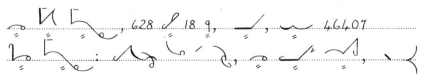

628 18 9, 46407

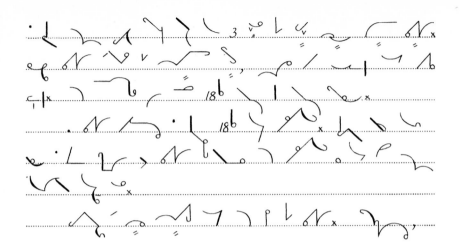

UNIT 2

VOCABULARY BUILDER

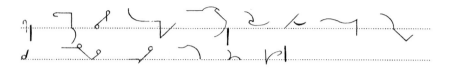

Key

treated courtesy hesitate factory accomplished ordinary recommend minute airport agents experts countries entire estimate outlined

SPECIAL OUTLINES

anybody .... nobody ....

TRANSCRIPTION POINTER

A rubber band or clip should be used to separate the used from the unused pages of a shorthand notebook. This enables the stenographer to turn to the writing page without fumbling or loss of time.

1

Midwest .... La Salle .... Puerto Rico .... scheduled .... business men .... emergencies ....

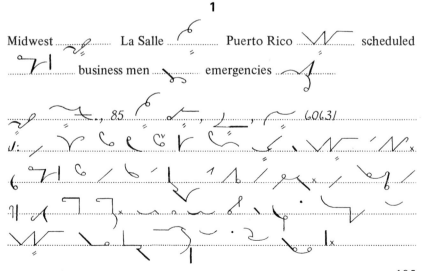

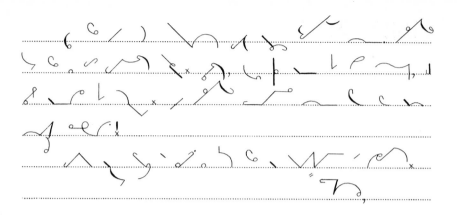

2

Harrisburg 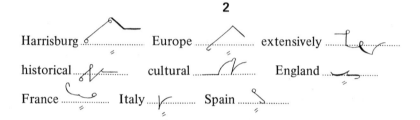 Europe extensively historical cultural England France Italy Spain

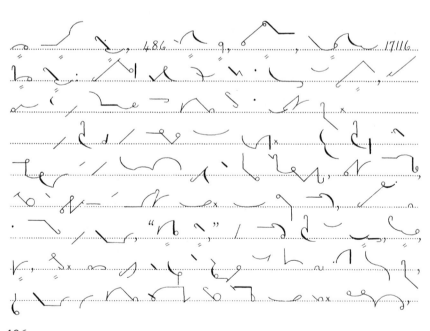

Donald 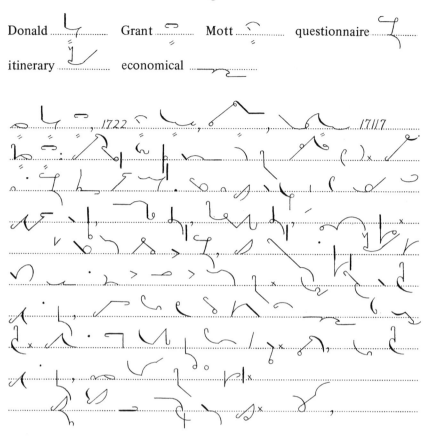 Grant Mott questionnaire

itinerary economical

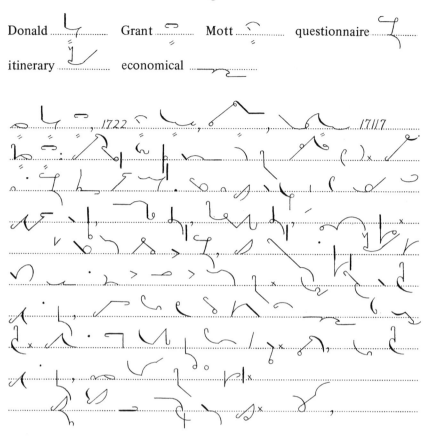

Does this letter have an enclosure?

CHALLENGE LETTER

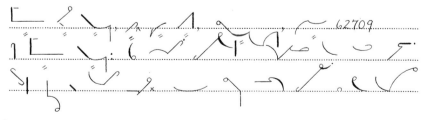

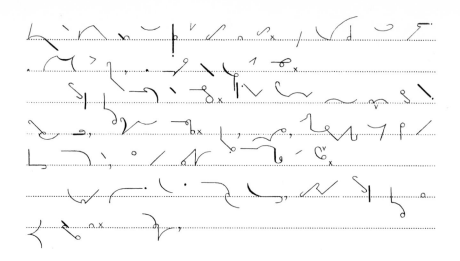

UNIT 3

VOCABULARY BUILDER

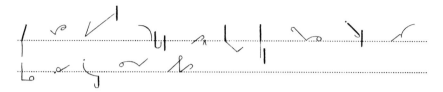

Key

jet islands chartered air-conditioned round depart dated permits
combined rental tickets concert confident smart restaurant

SPECIAL OUTLINES

similar .... familiar .... smaller ....

The boys were in the same club and wore *similar* jackets.

Are you *familiar* with the details of the trip?

My size is *smaller* than yours.

Note particularly the spelling of the last syllable in *similar* and *familiar*.

TRANSCRIPTION POINTER

The semicolon is not used very frequently. Its principal use is between
coordinate clauses which have commas:

The results of the poll, which reached us last week, show that you are
right; radio and television, our broadest media, are not being used
sufficiently.

1

Bucks County .... vacation .... Caribbean ....

neighboring .... sightseeing .... souvenirs ....

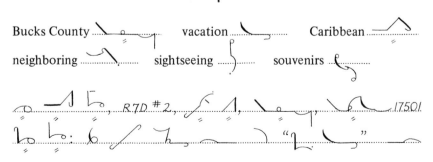

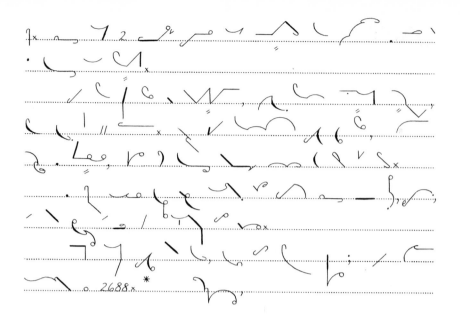

* In small towns, it is frequently unnecessary to dial an exchange.

2

Indianapolis ⌇⌇⌇⌇ faculty ⌇⌇⌇⌇ advisors ⌇⌇⌇⌇

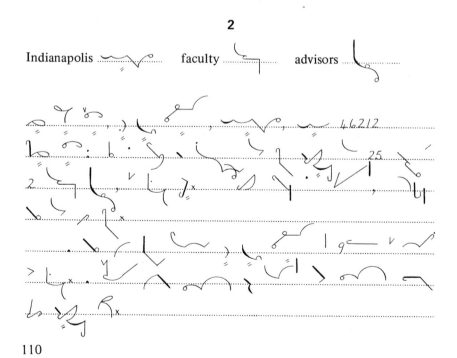

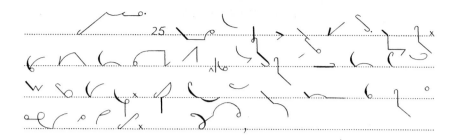

3

European  international ⁓⁓⁓ appreciative ⁓⁓

to make arrangements ⁓⁓

CHALLENGE LETTER

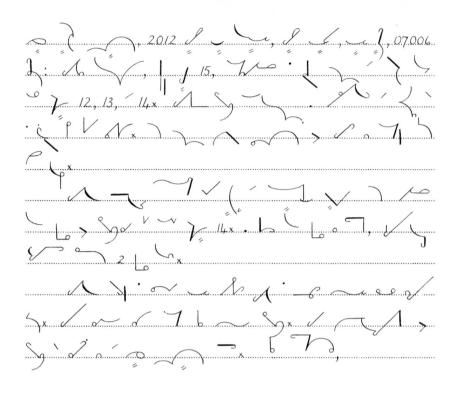

UNIT 4

VOCABULARY BUILDER

Key

instead cold winds frequent returned moderate greater requested extended scheduled events

SPECIAL OUTLINES

brochure ....🔗....... folder ....✓......

pamphlet ....🔗..... booklet ...✓.....

TRANSCRIPTION POINTER

The colon is used to introduce quotations. It is also used before listings:

Your agent in St. Louis sent us this message: "Ship all sale goods before August 10."

We have received the following items: 4 train cases, 6 hat boxes, and 12 flight bags.

This sentence may also be typed in the following way:

We have received the following items:

4 train cases

6 hat boxes

12 flight bags

1

Perkins 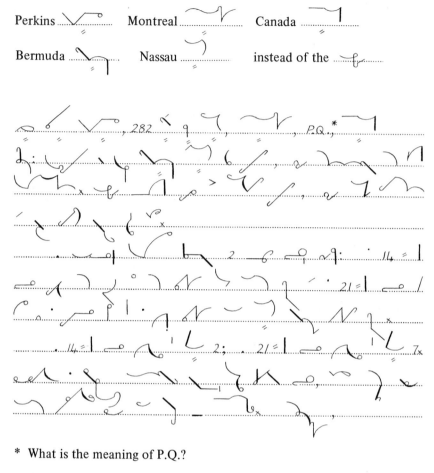 Montreal Canada

Bermuda Nassau instead of the

* What is the meaning of P.Q.?

2

Hunter more than we are concerned

privilege

114

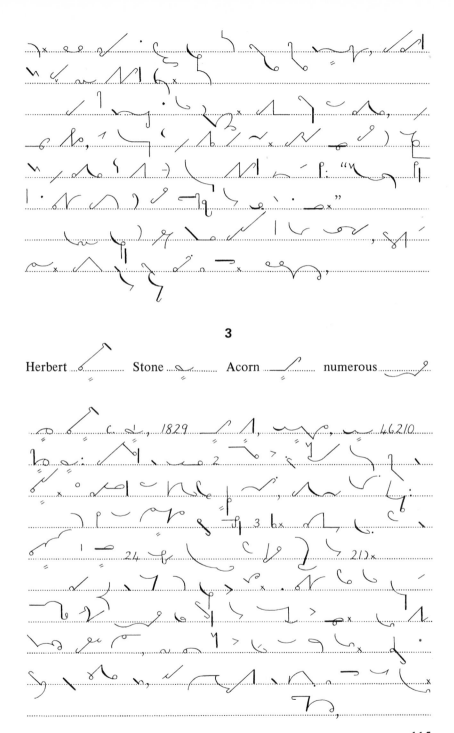

3

Herbert ....⌐........ Stone ...~........ Acorn ..../.......... numerous...../......

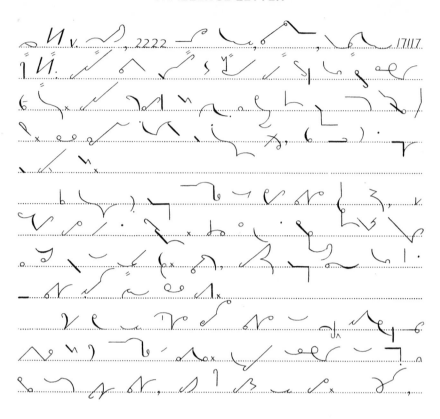

UNIT 5

VOCABULARY BUILDER

Key

limited worldwide protect protection flat index won't theft around quote lands submit arrangements

SPECIAL OUTLINES

favored 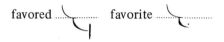 favorite

favoured (*adjective*) regarded with favor.

favourite (*adjective* or *noun*) person or thing regarded with favor or esteem. In sports, used to describe a likely winner.

Only a *favored* group will be allowed to participate.

This is my *favorite* television program.

This young golfer was the *favorite* in the tournament.

TRANSCRIPTION POINTER

The typist who can make neat corrections saves time and money for her employer. The first step in making a good correction is to remove the error. This may be done by erasing or by using one of the new chemical chalks. Experiment with both to see which gives you the least noticeable correction.

Errors should be corrected on the original copy and on the carbon copies so that an accurate record is placed in the file.

1

longer _____ more and more _____ International _____

routings _____ if it is _____ wherever _____

82-10 _____ 17109

2

Gabriel _____ dangerous _____ blowouts _____ fatigue _____

187 _____ 46216

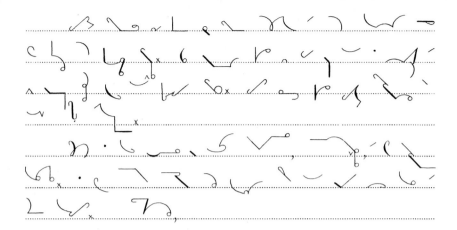

3

experienced  property  you may require

17507

CHALLENGE LETTER

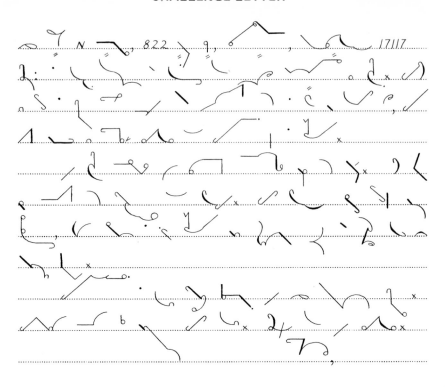

7

Banking

UNIT 1

VOCABULARY BUILDER

Key

Field require required clear cleared appear appeared Herald

SPECIAL OUTLINES

proof prove

proof (*noun*) evidence.

prove (*verb*) to demonstrate or establish as true by evidence.

The cancelled check was *proof* that he had bought the car.

You must *prove* ownership by showing a receipt or cancelled check.

TRANSCRIPTION POINTER

Quotation marks are used to enclose the exact wording of a statement or a question. They are also used to indicate the names of publications and titles:

"A rolling stone gathers no moss," is a much-quoted proverb.

Mary entered the office and asked, "Where shall we put the new machine?"

"The Globe" is a new school publication.

1

Merchants 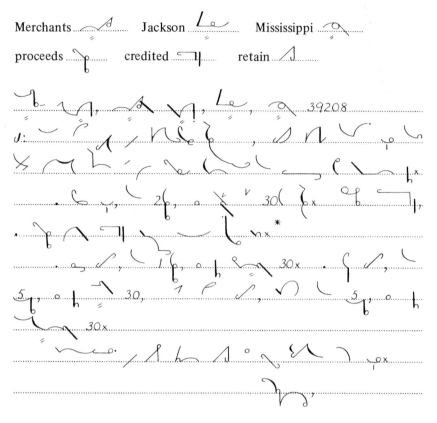 Jackson Mississippi

proceeds credited retain

39208

* What is the meaning of the phrase *under advice to you?*

2

Pacific Denver Colorado

promptness deed security transaction

legal department forwarded

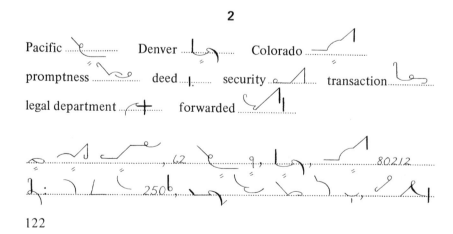

8.02.12

250

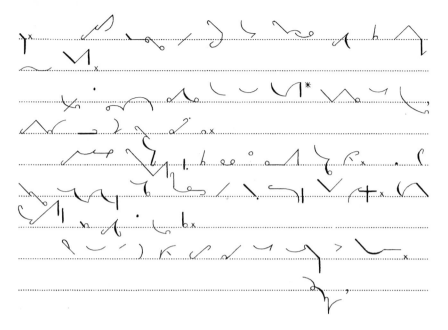

* What is the meaning of the word *valid*?

3

Yonkers 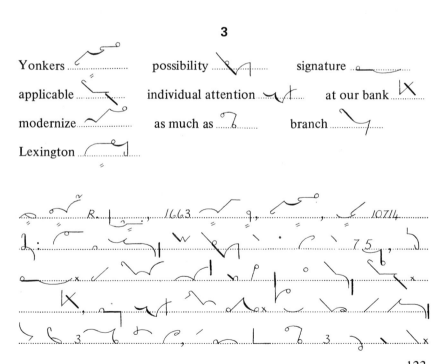 possibility _____ signature _____

applicable _____ individual attention _____ at our bank _____

modernize _____ as much as _____ branch _____

Lexington _____

CHALLENGE LETTER

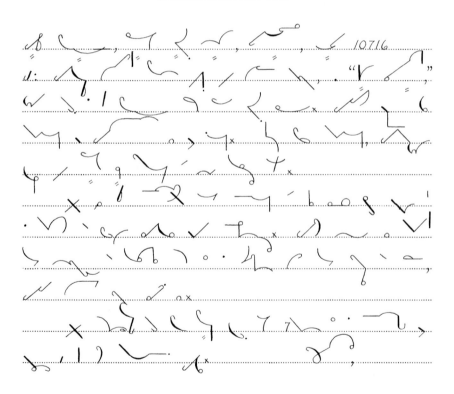

UNIT 2

VOCABULARY BUILDER

Key

Madam sound Soundview send sending middle modern

SPECIAL OUTLINES

indeed ....⌐⌐....   needed ....⌐⌐....   ended ....⌐⌐....

TRANSCRIPTION POINTER

The period and the comma are usually written before the closing quotation marks:

The new song, "Blue River," is a hit.
Be sure to end the message with the words "return receipt requested."

No space is left after the opening quotation marks or before the closing quotation marks.

1

Waring ....   Middle Village ....   finance

department ....   Stamford ....   approved ....

insurance ....

* When a sentence begins with a number, the number must be written in words.

** *Fee Title* insurance refers to insurance against deficiencies in the title of land.

2

in connection with the ⁓ᵧ accrued ⌐⌐|

escrow ⌐⌐ next week ⁓ₑ

* An escrow account is one in which money is held in trust for a special purpose.

126

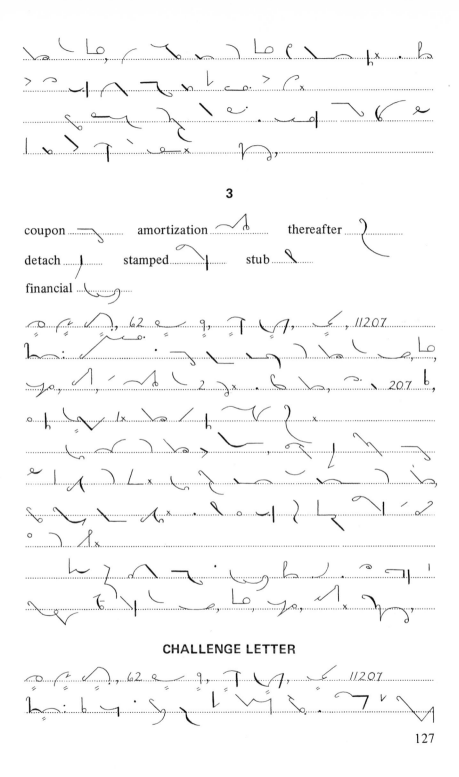

3

coupon .... amortization .... thereafter ....

detach .... stamped .... stub ....

financial ....

CHALLENGE LETTER

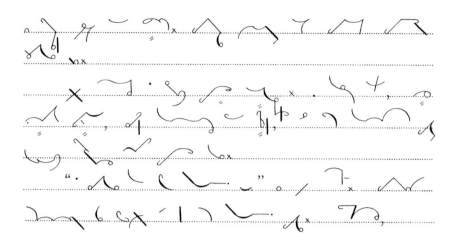

UNIT 3

VOCABULARY BUILDER

Key

installed prepared carried card billed

SPECIAL OUTLINES

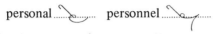

personal ....\>.... personnel ....\>....

personal (*adjective*) relates to one's private affairs.

personnel (*noun*) refers to a group of people employed in some service.

These *personal* matters should not be discussed during business hours.

The *personnel* in our Hartford branch is above average in attendance and accuracy.

TRANSCRIPTION POINTER

A common practice today is to use solid capital letters in place of quotation marks to indicate the names of publications. For example:

The DAILY HERALD is a popular newspaper.

The title of the book is A CENTURY OF PROGRESS.

However, statements or questions which are being quoted must be typed with quotation marks. (See Chapter 7–Unit 1.)

1

Pittsburgh .... in order to .... accurate ....

electronically .... bookkeeping .... our bank's ....

more than .... centralized .... depositors ....

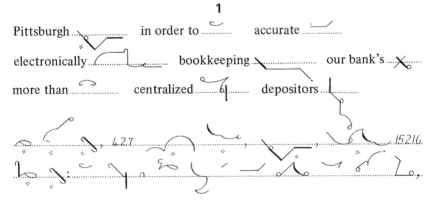

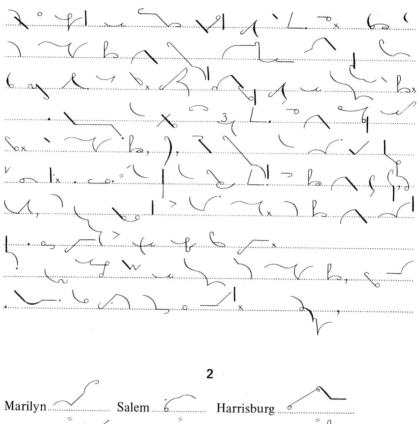

2

Marilyn ⁓⁓⁓ Salem ⁓⁓⁓ Harrisburg ⁓⁓⁓

which were ⁓⁓⁓ outstanding ⁓⁓⁓ transactions ⁓⁓⁓

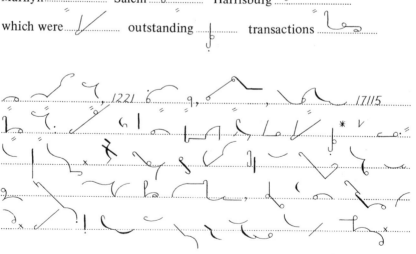

* What is meant by *outstanding checks*?

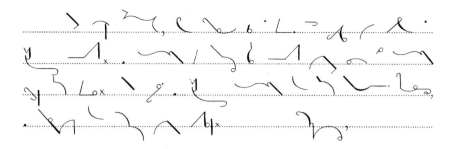

3

correspondent bank 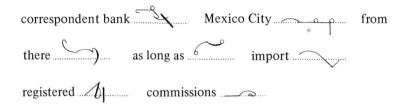 Mexico City _____ from

there _____ as long as _____ import _____

registered _____ commissions _____

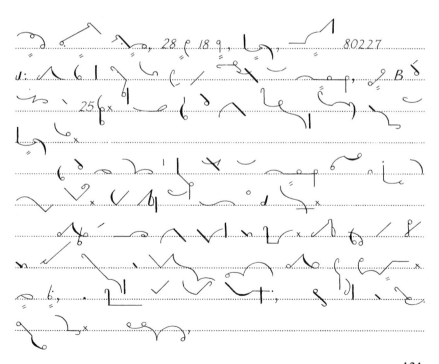

CHALLENGE LETTER

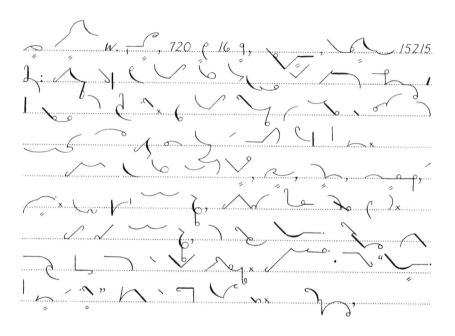

UNIT 4

VOCABULARY BUILDER

Key

under undertake confirmed confirmation your confirmation acquired

SPECIAL OUTLINES

appropriate (*adjective* or *verb*) ⌐⌐

adjective meaning is: suitable, fit, proper.

    This is an *appropriate* dress for the occasion.

verb meaning is: to take possession of, to set aside for a particular use.

    The government will *appropriate* the land and turn it into a public recreation area.

TRANSCRIPTION POINTER

    It is possible to eliminate many wasteful motions at the typewriter by utilizing those devices which promote greater efficiency and speed. The tabular stops, for example, should be preset for "average" letters so that you can automatically tabulate to the starting points for the date, paragraphs, and closing.

1

Trinity ...... Syracuse ...... cabled ...... previous ......

please arrange ...... for one year ......

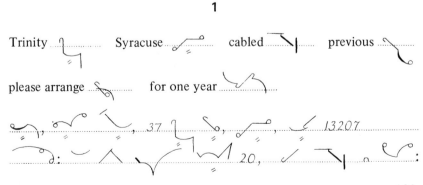

* What is a letter of credit?

2

Kelly ___ Donovan ___ encourage ___

preliminary arrangements ___ hereby ___ mature ___

negotiate ___

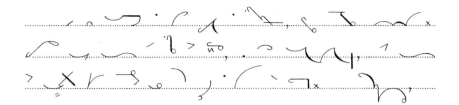

3

Lima  Peru unfortunately

in this matter actually guarantee

smaller companies please let us know

CHALLENGE LETTER

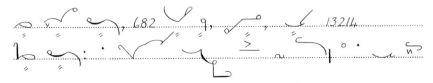

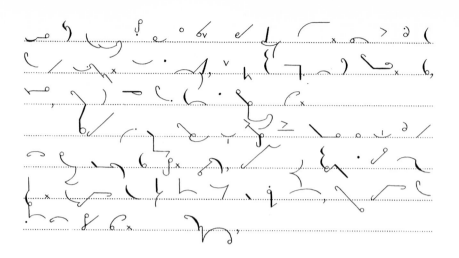

UNIT 5

VOCABULARY BUILDER

Key

filed understanding disappeared maturity old

SPECIAL OUTLINES

guaranty 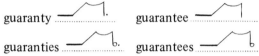 guarantee

guaranties guarantees

TRANSCRIPTION POINTER

The ZIP Code was established by the United States Post Office Department to identify a delivery unit. The units are associated with the major post offices through which mail is routed for delivery.

The country is divided into ten large areas and the first digit identifies the particular area. New York is in area 1, for example, and Utah is in area 8. The first three digits identify a major distribution point. The last two digits indicate the postal zone number.

ZIP Codes should follow the state in addresses.

1

Global _____ Grove _____ treasurer _____ cosigner _____

apparently _____ some arrangements _____ appreciative _____

cooperation _____

_____ 1836 _____ 9, _____ 10704 _____

d: _____ , _____ , _____ X

2

deductions 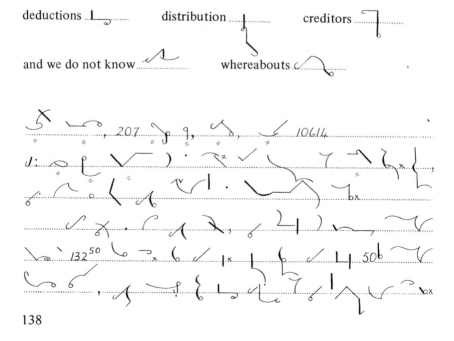 distribution creditors

and we do not know whereabouts

138

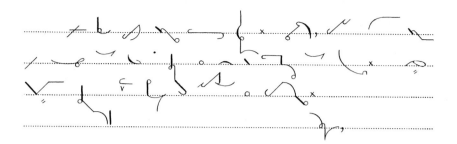

3

Northern 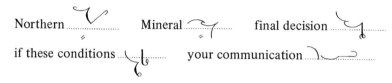 Mineral ⌐ final decision

if these conditions ⌐ your communication ⌐

CHALLENGE LETTER

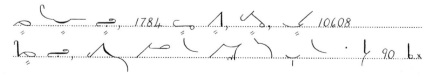

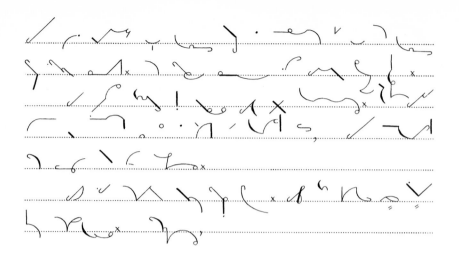

8

Office and Home Furnishings

UNIT 1

VOCABULARY BUILDER

Key

order filters feature after render interest wonder litter interfered introducing

SPECIAL OUTLINES

later latter

later means after the usual time; tardy.
latter means more recent; the end of a period.

    I will meet you *later* for dinner.
    The *latter* part of the twentieth century will show great scientific advances.

TRANSCRIPTION POINTER

    The apostrophe is used to form a possessive:
    The baker's hat is white.

    When a singular noun does not end in *s*, add the apostrophe and the *s* to the noun to show possession:

    The teacher's records are accurate. The school's reputation is excellent.

141

When a singular noun ends in *s*, the apostrophe is always added to form the possessive. If this is difficult to pronounce, the additional *s* may be omitted:

Charles's book is lost. BUT Mr. Hopkins' answer came too late.

1

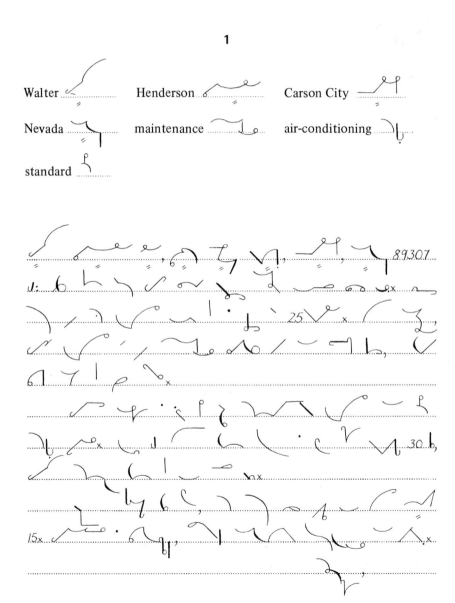

Walter   Henderson   Carson City

Nevada   maintenance   air-conditioning

standard

Fetterman 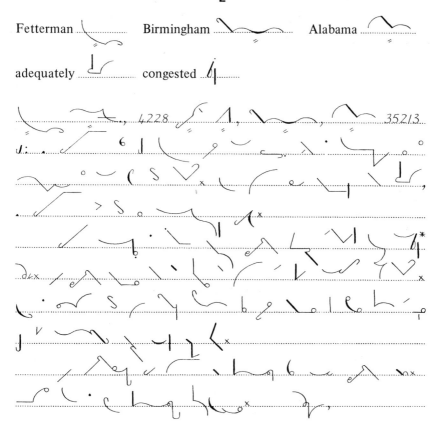 Birmingham .... Alabama ....

adequately .... congested ....

* What is the meaning of *congested*?

3

Carpenter .... Montgomery .... weeks ago ....
vacuum .... several times .... designed ....
ordinary .... September ....

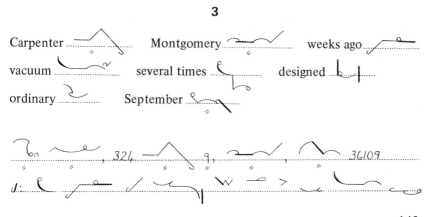

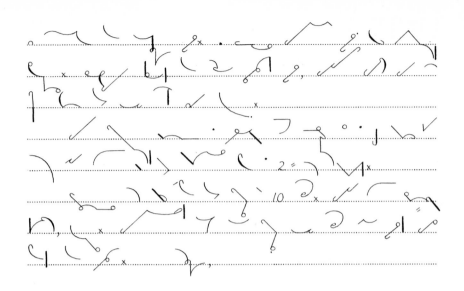

CHALLENGE LETTER

UNIT 2

VOCABULARY BUILDER

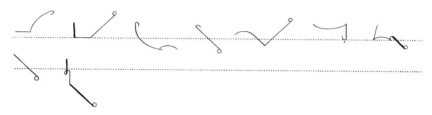

Key

calendar decorators furthermore planters importers entertaining
chambers painters distributors

SPECIAL OUTLINES

feature .‿‿‿‿.   future .‿‿‿‿.

TRANSCRIPTION POINTER

When a plural noun ends in *s*, only the apostrophe is added to form the possessive:

The pupils' activities in clubs are supervised.
There are doctors' offices in this building.

Plurals which do not end in *s* add an apostrophe and *s* to form the possessive:

Women's hats are on sale today.
The manager must solve the salesmen's problems.

1

tasteful ‿‿‿   furnishings ‿‿‿   decorations ‿‿‿

interior ‿‿‿   designers ‿‿‿   gratitude ‿‿‿

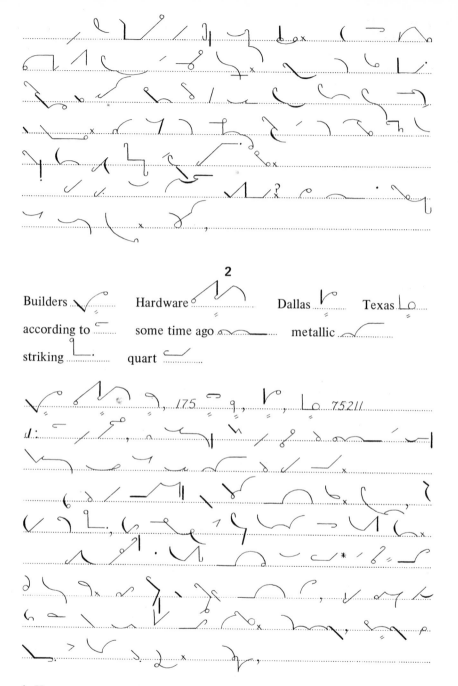

2

Builders ⌇⌇⌇⌇ Hardware ⌇⌇⌇⌇ Dallas ⌇⌇⌇⌇ Texas ⌇⌇⌇⌇

according to ⌇⌇⌇⌇ some time ago ⌇⌇⌇⌇ metallic ⌇⌇⌇⌇

striking ⌇⌇⌇⌇ quart ⌇⌇⌇⌇

* How many quarts in a half-gallon?

Cactus  Houston   planters

Gift Department   pottery   they are

imports

CHALLENGE LETTER

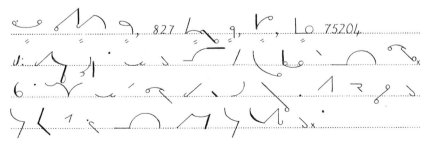

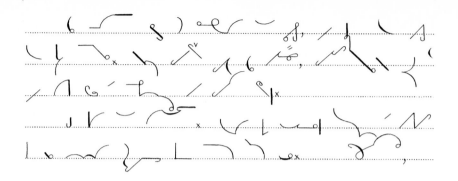

UNIT 3

VOCABULARY BUILDER

Key

typewriters duplicators central wonderful. *Phrases:* if there is another company

SPECIAL OUTLINES

then ......(..... than ....(.....

then (*adverb*) meaning at that time; next; consequently.

than (*conjunction*) is used after adjectives and adverbs of comparative degree.

Finish your homework. *Then* you may go to the movies.

It is easier said *than* done.

TRANSCRIPTION POINTER

The possessive of an abbreviation is formed by adding the apostrophe and *s*; when the abbreviation ends in *s*, only the apostrophe is added:

You must have a C.P.A.'s audit.

Pope Bros.' store is closed.

1

Porter .... Baxter .... Cumberland ....

Fort Worth .... it is possible .... needless ....

approximately ....

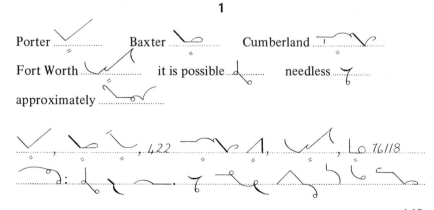

(YU) 6-8247.*

* Telephone exchanges may be typed as YUkon 6-8247 or YUKON 6-8247. Capitalization of at least the first two letters helps the caller when dialing.

2

Empire 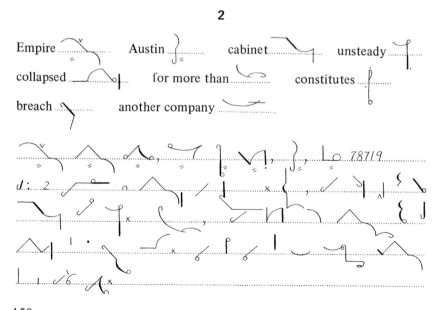 Austin cabinet unsteady

collapsed for more than constitutes

breach another company

78719

J.: 2

150

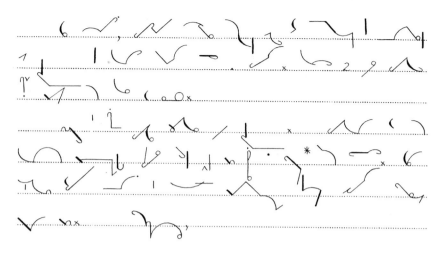

*To breach an agreement is to fail to live up to the conditions and terms.

3

Appliance Corporation 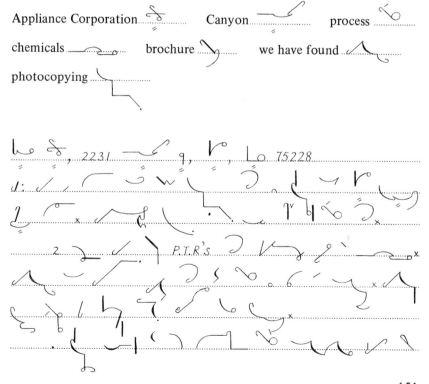 Canyon process

chemicals brochure we have found

photocopying

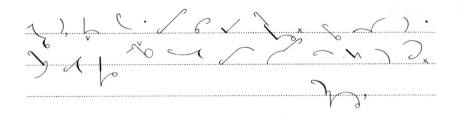

CHALLENGE LETTER

UNIT 4

VOCABULARY BUILDER

Key

builders timber contractors refrigerators feature featured

SPECIAL OUTLINES

in order to ⌣ in order ⌣ in order that ⌣(

column ⌢ volume ⌣ film ⌣

TRANSCRIPTION POINTER

The small business envelope (6½ inches x 3⅝ inches) is generally used when only one sheet of stationery is to be folded for mailing.

If there is an enclosure or a letter of more than one page, the large business envelope (9½ inches x 4⅛ inches) should be used.

The envelope address of the letter should be the same styling as the inside address. However, since the post office prefers envelopes to be double spaced, the addresses will vary in this regard.

Special information (AIR MAIL, SPECIAL DELIVERY) should be typed two spaces under the stamp on the top, right-hand corner of the envelope.

Use the ZIP Code for your address on all your correspondence. If you keep an address list, note the ZIP Codes for addresses with which you correspond frequently. Be sure the ZIP Code number is correct and that it is accurately typed.

1

Linder 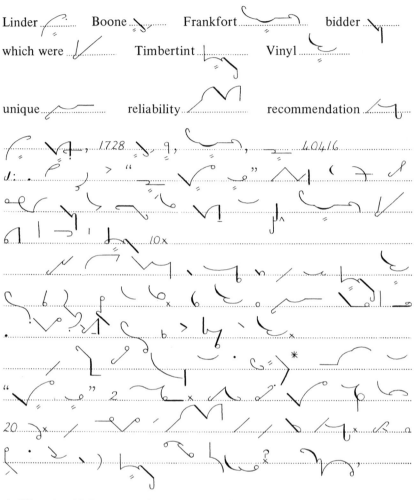   Boone   Frankfort   bidder

which were   Timbertint   Vinyl

unique   reliability   recommendation

1728   4.0416

10 x

* Why should *front-page* be hyphenated?

2

acquired   resistant   scuff   scratches

1728   4.0416

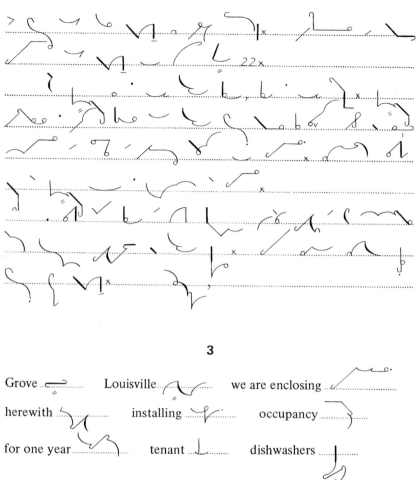

3

Grove  Louisville we are enclosing

herewith installing occupancy

for one year tenant dishwashers

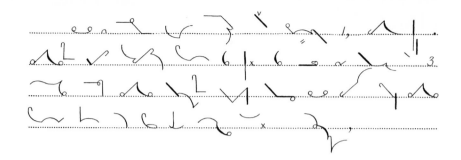

CHALLENGE LETTER

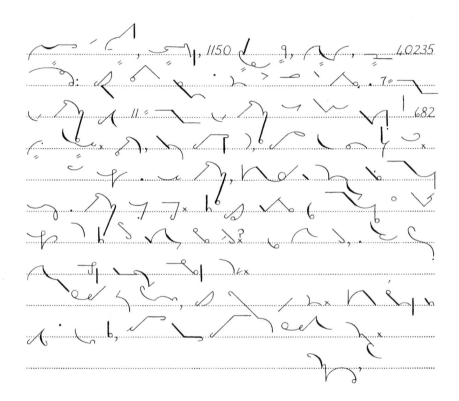

UNIT 5

VOCABULARY BUILDER

Key

binder folders venture afternoon. *Phrase*: in your letter

SPECIAL OUTLINES

memorandum ⌒⌒⌒ memo ⌒⌒⌒

TRANSCRIPTION POINTER

When mail is to be enclosed in a window envelope, the address on the enclosure is of the greatest importance since it must be seen clearly through the window.

When the stationery is folded, the lower edge is first folded up about ⅓ the length of the sheet; the upper edge is then folded *back* of the first fold so that the inside address remains on the *outside*; the letter is inserted into the envelope with the address toward the front of the envelope.

The address can then be seen clearly through the window.

1

New England ⌒⌒ stationery ⌒ Coliseum ⌒

commitments ⌒ questionnaire ⌒ visitors ⌒

accommodations ⌒ Columbus ⌒

⌒ , 1685 ⌒ 9, ⌒ , ⌒ 06624

⌒ ⌒ ⌒ ⌒ ⌒ ⌒ ⌒ ⌒

157

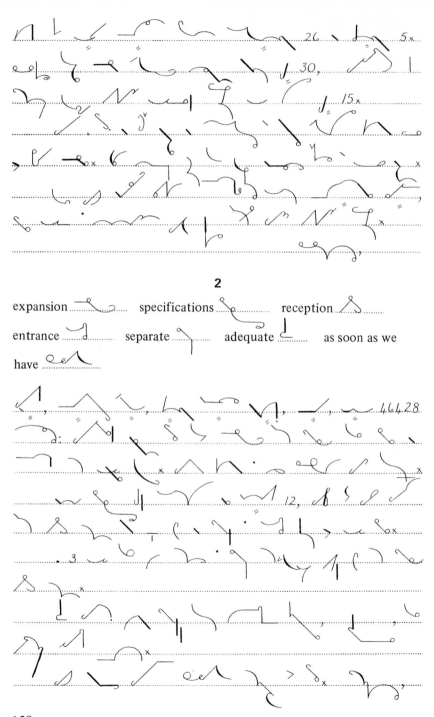

2

expansion .... specifications .... reception ....

entrance .... separate .... adequate .... as soon as we

have ....

appliance 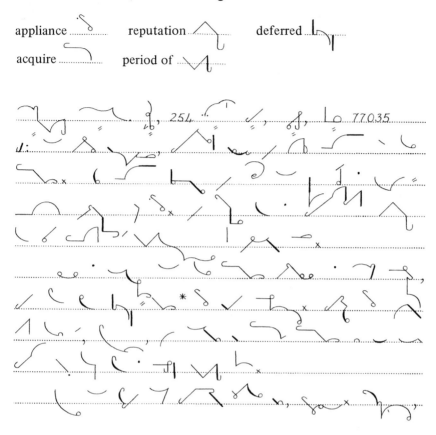 reputation deferred

acquire period of

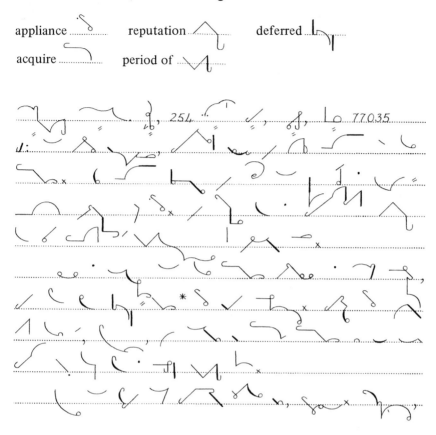

254 *77035*

* What is a deferred-payment plan?

CHALLENGE LETTER

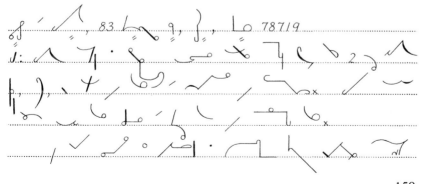

83 *78719*

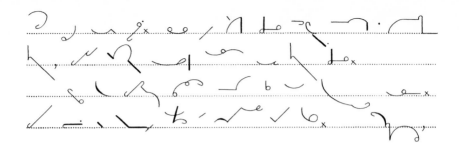

9

Education, Schools, On-the-job Training

UNIT 1

VOCABULARY BUILDER

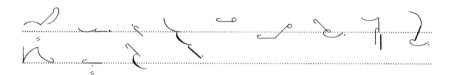

Key

Marshall including complete favorably class clearance personally entitled originally telephone Clay approval

SPECIAL OUTLINES

till ⌐⌐⌐ until ⌐

TRANSCRIPTION POINTER

Good posture at the typewriter is important for good production and for the reduction of fatigue.

Always try to sit erect, with feet on the floor and your body bent slightly forward. Keep the upper arms and elbows near your body. Let your wrists slant upward to the machine, but do not let them touch the machine. Keep your eyes on the copy.

1

.Bookbindery.... Atlanta.... Georgia....

apprenticeship.... aptitude.... as we are....

next week.... Clark....

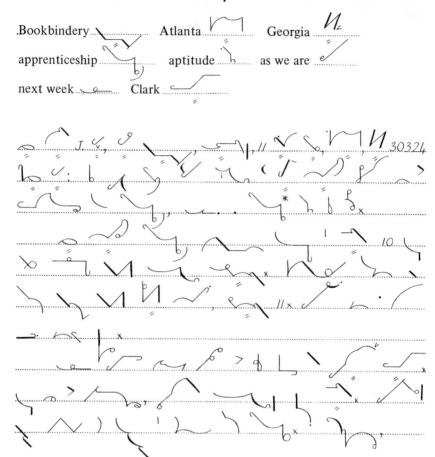

* What is an apprentice?

2

candidates.... enrollment.... conform....

application forms.... union....

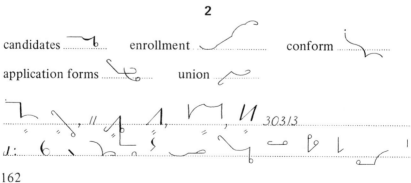

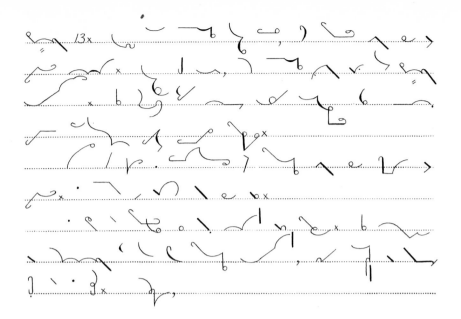

3

Textiles ⌐ₚᵥₒ   Savannah ⌒   Bureau ⟍⟋

registration ⤴   trends ᴦ   without delay ⟨

163

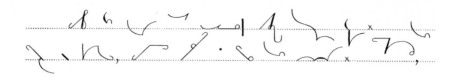

CHALLENGE LETTER

UNIT 2

VOCABULARY BUILDER

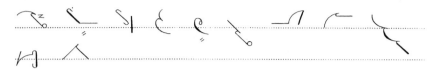

Key

employees Black planned thoughtful Civil pupils college local
favorable children reply

SPECIAL OUTLINES

explanation ⟍⟋ exception ⟍

TRANSCRIPTION POINTER

Review the following uses of the comma:

In a series:

The pupils gave a party for the class, for the teachers, for the
parents, and for the administration.

In direct address:

Do you think, Robert, that you will be with us on Saturday?

With introductory words like "well" and "yes":

Yes, it is early enough to enter the contest.

With dates:

The dance will be held on Thursday, March 16, at the Hotel
America.

1

Omaha _____ Nebraska _____ for many years _____

hesitated _____ junior _____

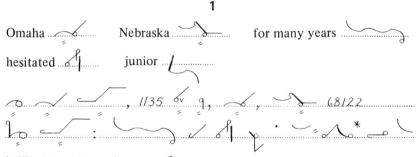

* What is an in-service course?

2

Platt ⌐⌐⌐⌐⌐⌐⌐⌐ Blakeley ⌐⌐⌐⌐⌐⌐⌐ Society ⌐⌐⌐⌐⌐⌐⌐

inspiration ⌐⌐⌐⌐⌐⌐ look forward ⌐⌐⌐⌐⌐⌐

68114

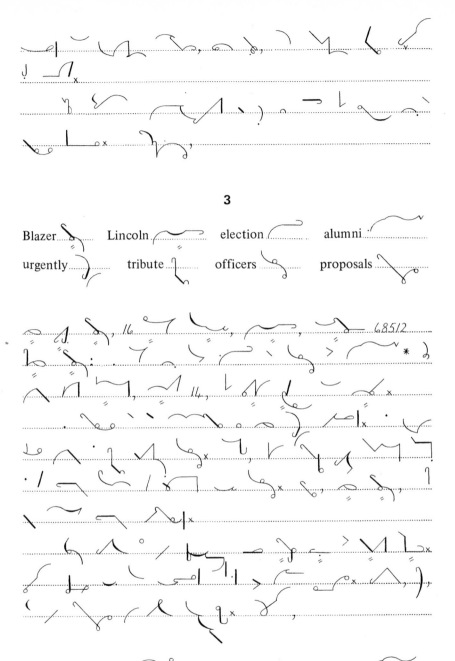

3

Blazer Lincoln election alumni

urgently tribute officers proposals

* alumnus (*male*) college graduate; alumna (*female*)
alumni (plural of *alumnus*) ; alumnae (plural of *alumna*)

CHALLENGE LETTER

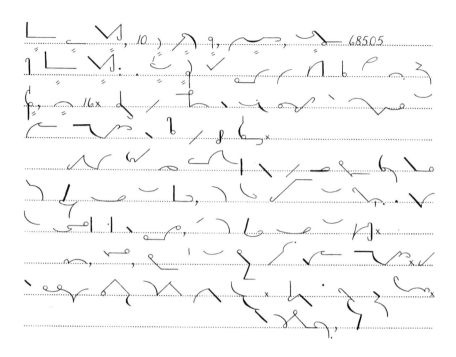

UNIT 3

VOCABULARY BUILDER

Key

assembly obligation vital collective specialists samples

SPECIAL OUTLINES

stationary ....ε........ stationery .ε........

stationary means standing still.
stationery means paper for letter writing.

TRANSCRIPTION POINTER

The dash is a more emphatic mark of punctuation than the comma, the semicolon, or the colon. Under certain conditions it can be used instead of any one of these marks.

It may be used instead of a comma for more emphatic separation from the rest of the sentence:

We are determined that our pupils — as well as their teachers — shall receive a fair decision.

It may be used instead of a semicolon with an example or explanation:

The applications will be accepted for local colleges — for example, New York University, Long Island University, and Brooklyn College.

1

Nashville ....⌒.... Tennessee ....L....⌐.... this week ....⌐....

next week ....⌐....

⌐ ╱ ₋₀, 107 ⌐ ⌐ ⌐ ╱ ⌐ L 37219

╰ ₋₀: ╱ ⌐ ⌐ L L , ╱ ⌐ ⌐ ⌐x

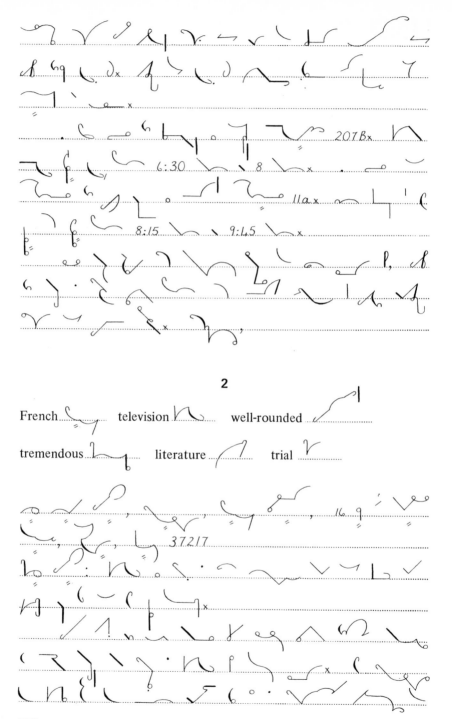

2

French _____ television _____ well-rounded _____

tremendous _____ literature _____ trial _____

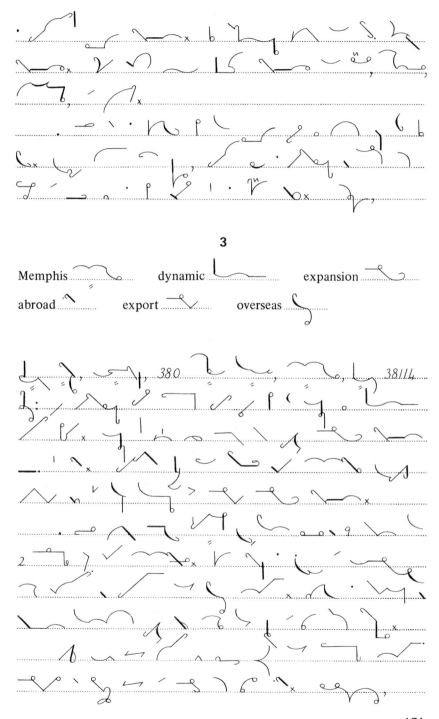

3

Memphis   dynamic   expansion

abroad   export   overseas

CHALLENGE LETTER

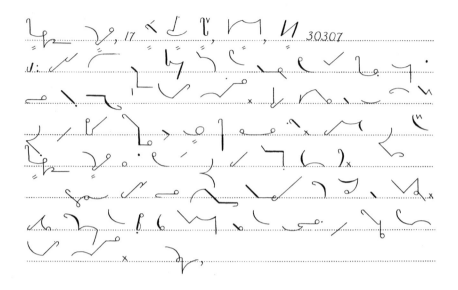

UNIT 4

VOCABULARY BUILDER

Key

helpful enclosed available challenging clothing eligible initial confidentially complying trouble periodically

SPECIAL OUTLINES

already ⌄⌐ all right ⌄⌐

TRANSCRIPTION POINTER

The dash has several uses of its own.

(a) It is used before a summary of words:
Radios, televisions, phonographs – all were on sale.

(b) It is used when repeating for emphasis:
You are the teacher – the teacher who won the award.

(c) It is used before an afterthought, or when there is hesitation:
We'll meet you on Saturday – perhaps in the afternoon.

1

English Department _____ inasmuch as _____ semester _____

will you _____ appreciate _____ up to date _____

_____ 15 _____ _____ 3.7.2.16

J: _____ x _____

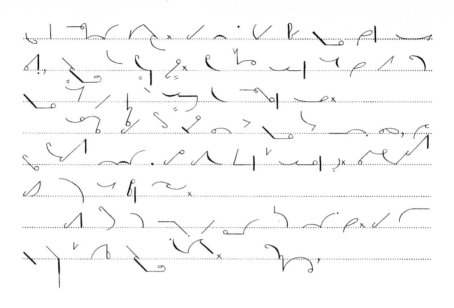

2

approximately 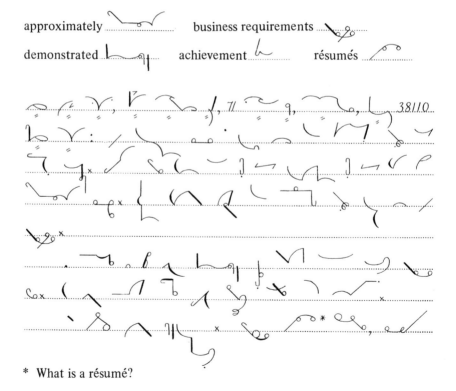 business requirements

demonstrated achievement résumés

* What is a résumé?

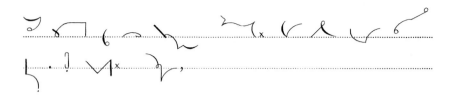

3

we appreciate 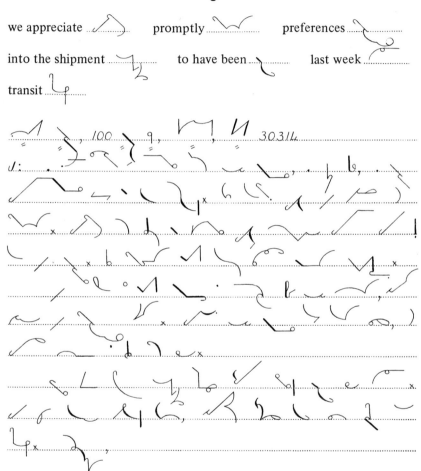 promptly preferences

into the shipment to have been last week

transit

CHALLENGE LETTER

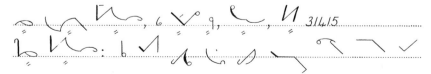

175

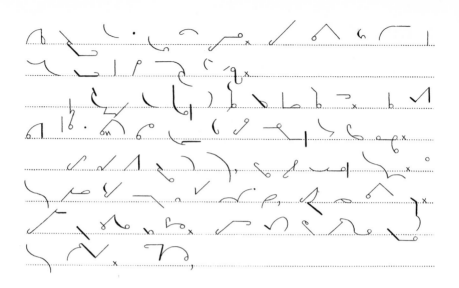

UNIT 5

VOCABULARY BUILDER

Key

privilege grateful pamphlets legal pleasant technical explore fleet

SPECIAL OUTLINES

precede ⌇ proceed ⌇

Precede (*verb*) means to go before.

Proceed (*verb*) is to continue to advance.

TRANSCRIPTION POINTER

Review the following uses of the comma:

(*a*) There is no comma with a restrictive phrase:
The pupil who received the award is my cousin.

(*b*) Use commas with a nonrestrictive phrase:
John Brooks, who received the award, is my cousin.

(*c*) Use commas to separate main clauses joined by *and*, *but*, etc.:
Last week we bought curtains and rugs for the house, and this week we completed all the painting.

(*d*) Use commas with parenthetic words:
We believe, therefore, that you should be with us at the dinner.

177

1

ranks ⏤ forefront ⏤ facilities ⏤ wholly ⏤

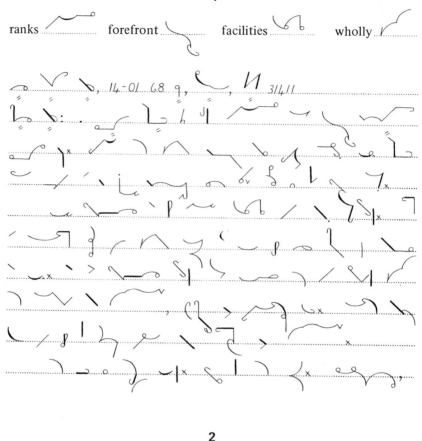

2

Blair ⏤ Clyde ⏤ indebted ⏤ extensive ⏤

legal department ⏤ relationship ⏤

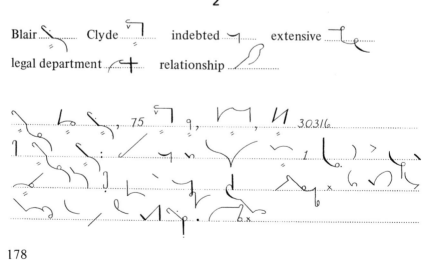

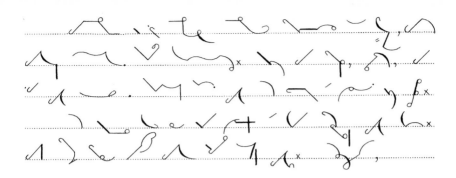

3

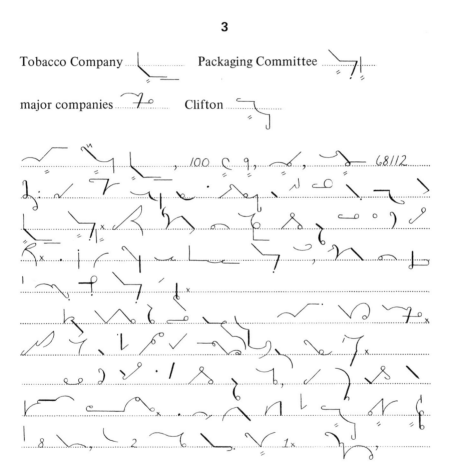

Tobacco Company   Packaging Committee

major companies   Clifton

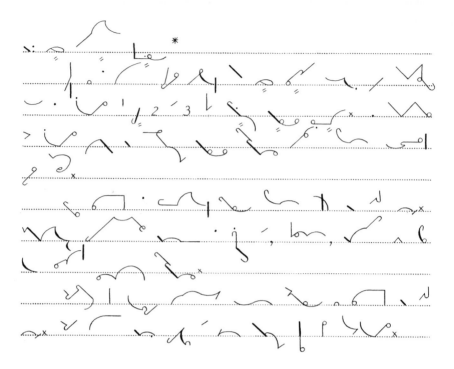

* This is an interoffice memo. When is it used?

10

Review

UNIT 1

VOCABULARY BUILDER

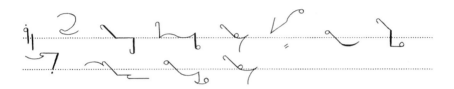

Key

considered machinery breakdown tremendous presently Charles spring products encouraging impractical superintendents personnel

SPECIAL OUTLINES

separate ⌐ separately ⌐ separation ⌐

TRANSCRIPTION POINTER

To avoid "flying" capitals, remember to hold the shift key down firmly until the capital letter has been struck. Then release the shift key immediately and return the finger to the guide key. When typing a series of uppercase letters, use the shift lock to save time.

1

Topeka 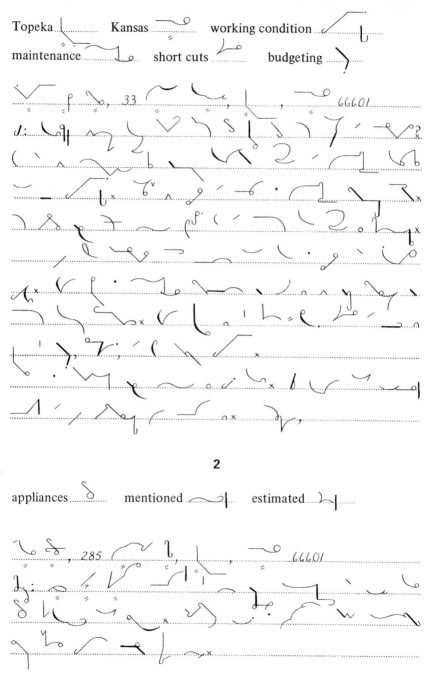 Kansas working condition

maintenance short cuts budgeting

2

appliances mentioned estimated

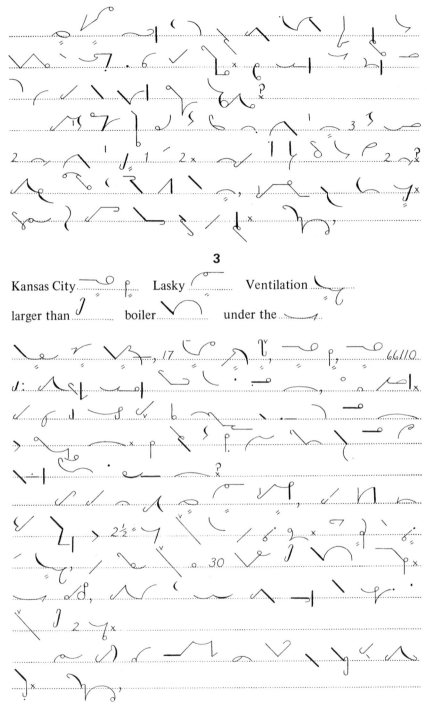

3

Kansas City ⌒ ρ Lasky ⌒ Ventilation ⌒

larger than ♩ boiler ⌄⌒ under the ⌒

6.6110

2½ 30

183

UNIT 2

VOCABULARY BUILDER

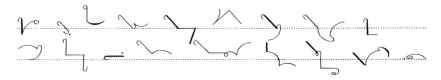

Key

drills printing strong prevent breakage sharp brochure professional
direct measure attractive eager prime approximately auditorium
obstructions boulevard consumer

SPECIAL OUTLINES

number-ed .... ＼ .... ＼|. *Phrase:* number of .... ＼.

TRANSCRIPTION POINTER

Remember to keep your eyes on the printed copy when using the line
space lever or carriage return. On a manual machine, keep your palm down
and your index finger against the carriage return lever. Your right hand
should remain on the guide keys. The left hand should be returned to the
guide keys as quickly as possible after completing the carriage throw.

On an electric typewriter, the carriage is returned automatically by
depressing the carriage return key.

Good posture helps to effect a smooth carriage return and to obtain an
even left-hand margin.

1

binderies ....   by our company ....   chipping ....

we are in a position ....   workmanship ....

assorted ....

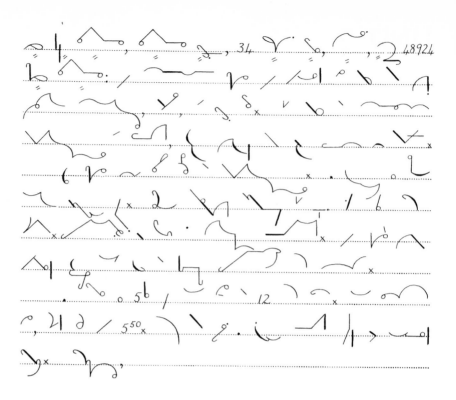

2

accountants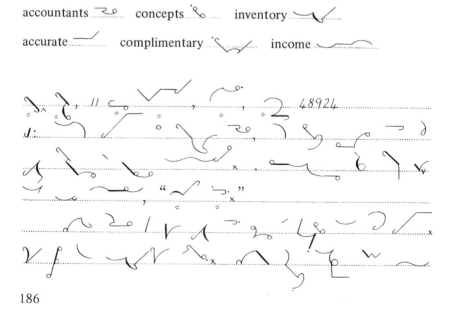

accurate ⁀   concepts ⸰₀   complimentary ⌣∕   inventory ⌣∕   income ⌣‿

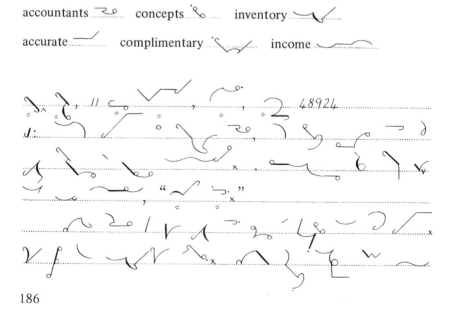

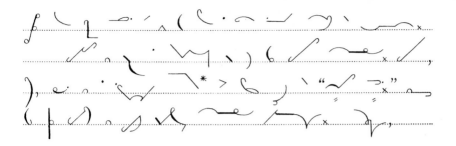

* What is a complimentary copy?

3

Cincinnati 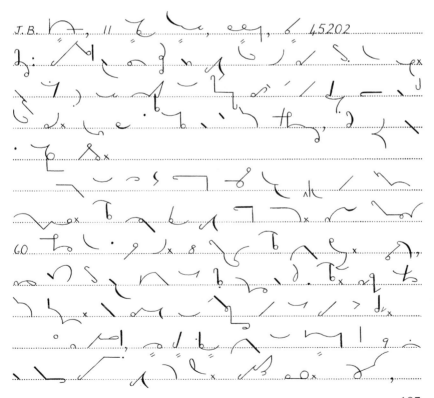 Ohio merchandise

surroundings costumes

J.B. ... , ll ... , ... , 45202

60

CHALLENGE LETTER

UNIT 3

VOCABULARY BUILDER

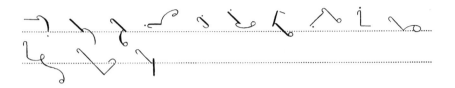

Key

covering before brothers congratulations brand banners jobbers
wrappers contract premises transfers preparation provide

SPECIAL OUTLINES

its .... it's ....

its is a possessive word which means *belonging to.*
it's is a contraction which means *it is.*
    We picked that hat because of *its* color.
    It's going to rain this afternoon.

TRANSCRIPTION POINTER

    Review the following uses of the semicolon:

    (*a*)   Use the semicolon between two independent clauses when the
conjuction has been omitted:
        The pupils were satisfied; the teachers were not.

    (*b*)   Use the semicolon to separate independent clauses in a compound
sentence when either or both clauses contain other punctuation:
        The party, after much planning, was a success; however, we were
      very tired.

1

Pierre   South Dakota   covering

authorization   Frazer   delinquent

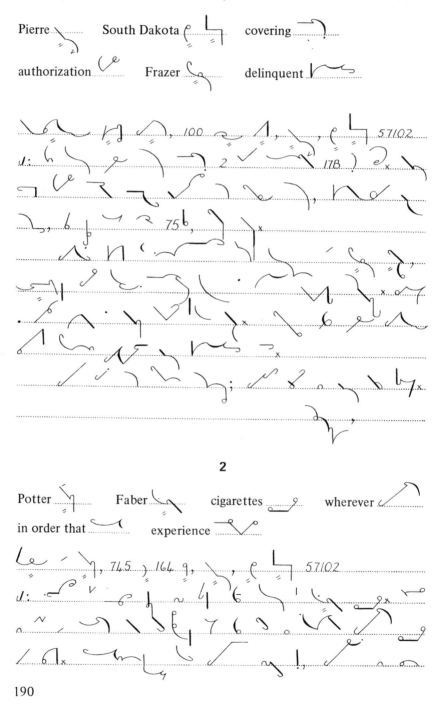

100.   5.7.10.2.   2   17.B.   75.

2

Potter   Faber   cigarettes   wherever

in order that   experience

74.5   164.   5.7.10.2

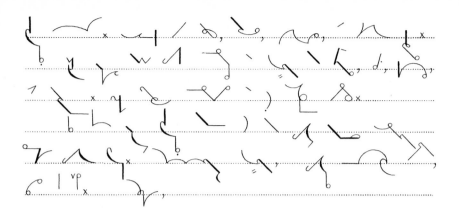

3

we have received 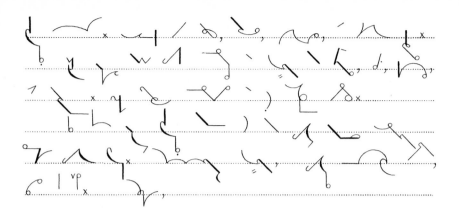 welfare negotiations

institute realty

CHALLENGE LETTER

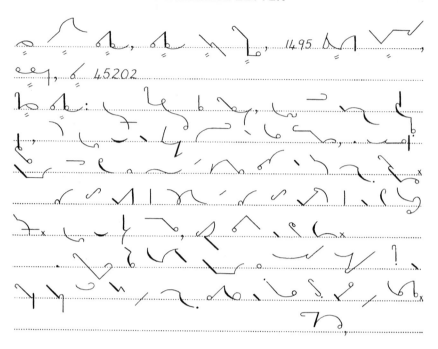

UNIT 4

VOCABULARY BUILDER

Key

engineers courteous effort branch group merger industries district Virginia comfortably

SPECIAL OUTLINES

whose .... who's ....

Whose (pronoun) shows the possessive of *who.*
Who's is the contracted form of *who is.*
    We know *whose* coat was lost.
    Who's responsible for this disturbance?

TRANSCRIPTION POINTER

Review the following uses of the colon:

(*a*)   Use the colon after *the following* or *as follows* and *these*, etc.:
    The following people did not attend the meeting: Rose, Mildred, and Frances.
    The essential points were these: the course takes one term, it meets weekly, and it carries two credits.

(*b*)   Use a colon if the introducing word is implied:
    Lost: one grey French poodle in the vicinity of 969 Broadway.

1

possibilities .... chewing .... to impose ....

reopen the ....

.........., 400 ...., ..., 48,924.

.........!

193

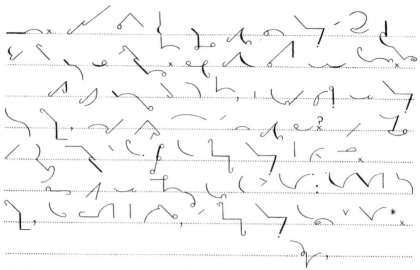

* What is meant by "eye appeal"?

2

staffed 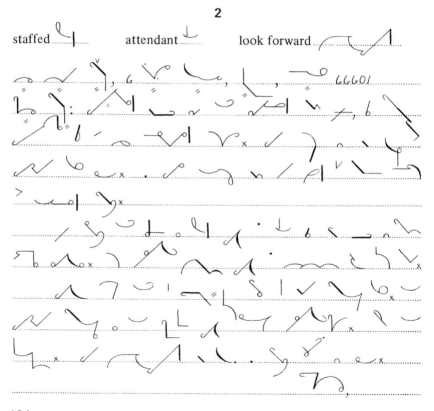   attendant   look forward

Shoreham 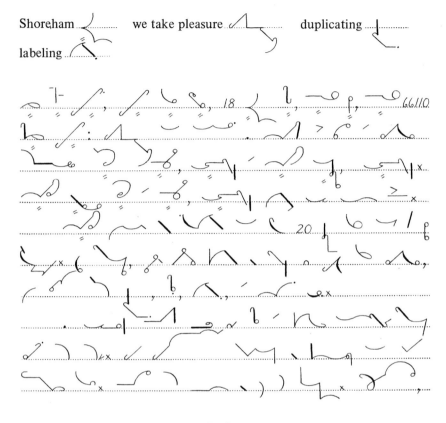 we take pleasure duplicating labeling

CHALLENGE LETTER

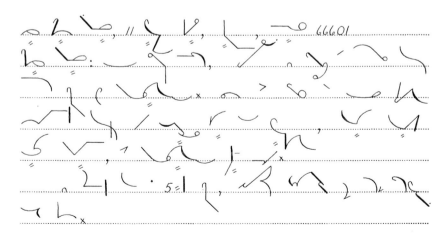

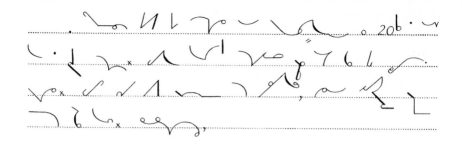

UNIT 5

VOCABULARY BUILDER

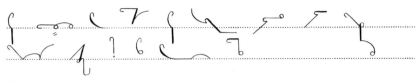

Key

third Christmas every cordially thread fabric recourse regret procedures promotional registration trying authors overcome graduates

SPECIAL OUTLINES

perhaps ⟍ purpose ⟍⟋⟍

TRANSCRIPTION POINTER

Review the following uses of the apostrophe:

(*a*)   Use an apostrophe with possessives. Place the apostrophe before the *s* for the singular and after the *s* for the plural:

It was Mary's hat that was found in the girls' locker room.

(*b*)   Use an apostrophe in a contraction:

Who's going with us?

Who hasn't heard of the school?

(*c*)   Use an apostrophe with plurals of letters, figures, etc.:

We have some dresses left in 8's and 10's.

1

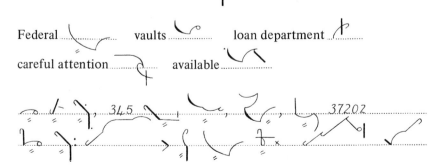

Federal ⟍ vaults ⟍ loan department ⟋

careful attention ⟍ available ⟍

345 37202

2

defect .... weaving .... defective ....

* What is the meaning of *recourse*?

198

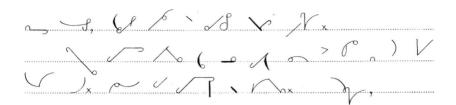

Small Business  current business
contemplate  their own businesses  hasn't

CHALLENGE LETTER

11 Finance

UNIT 1

VOCABULARY BUILDER

Key

achieve definite graphs define Buff gift wife life proof serving

SPECIAL OUTLINES

Note the use of the F and V hook in the following words:

private ......🖎.....   profit ......🖎.....   provide ......🖎.....

TRANSCRIPTION POINTER

Keep your eyes on your shorthand notes when you are transcribing. It is very easy to lose your place if you look back and forth.

Read through the whole letter before you begin to type. Note special punctuation and paragraphing.

Always verify the spelling of unusual names of people and places and write them clearly in longhand. Also note enclosures and the number of copies needed.

1

Boise 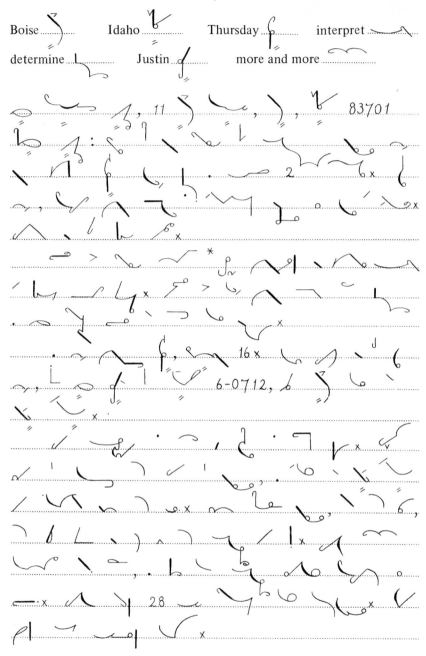 Idaho Thursday interpret

determine Justin more and more

83701

2

16 x

6-07.12,

28

* *market* refers to the stock market.

202

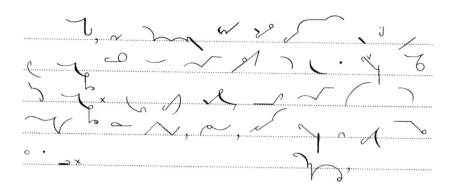

2

earnings ⌐⌐⌐   becoming ⌐⌐⌐   trusted ⌐⌐⌐   broker ⌐⌐⌐

guidance ⌐⌐⌐   common ⌐⌐⌐

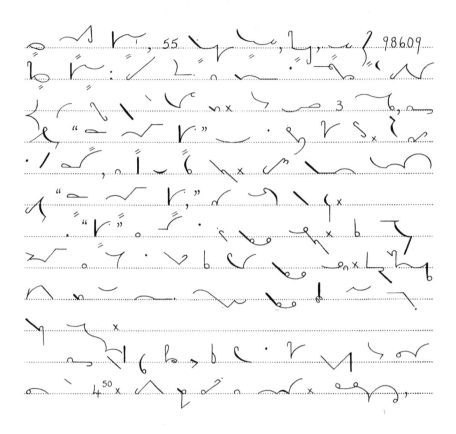

UNIT 2

VOCABULARY BUILDER

Key

defend defense advances brief reserve dividend

SPECIAL OUTLINES

Note the use of the F or V hook in:

serve ......✗...... serves ......✗......

Compare with: service ..✗✗..... survey ..✗✗...

TRANSCRIPTION POINTER

Always write out numbers when they begin a sentence:
Fifty girls attended the dance.

Always write decimals in figures. Never insert a comma:
7.256   21.4857638

When you write out fractions, include the word *and* between the whole number and the fraction:
three and three-fifths.

1

Hartford ....✗...... freedom ..✗...... federal government ..✗......

science...✗..... maturity ..✗.....

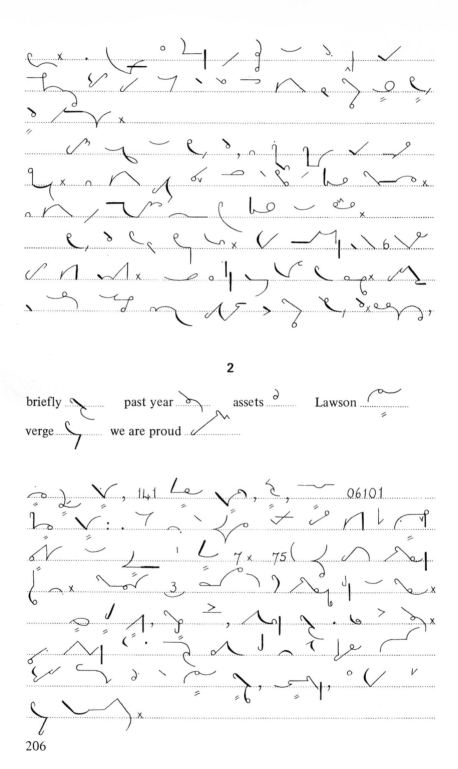

2

briefly

past year

assets

Lawson

verge

we are proud

06101

7 x 75

3

206

3

that you were _____ five million dollars _5_ _____ more than _____

yield _____

..., 14) 65 9, ..., 06101

5

75

27. 635   6

275

CHALLENGE LETTER

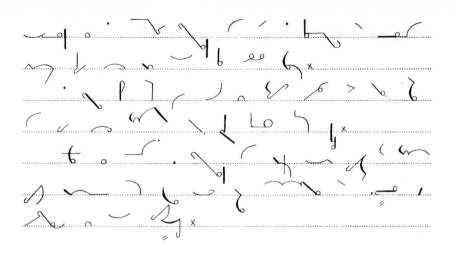

UNIT 3

VOCABULARY BUILDER

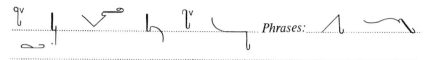

Key

strive defeat paragraphs defer drive effective. *Phrases:* rate of
number of stock of

SPECIAL OUTLINES

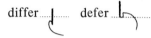

differ ⌐ defer ⌐

differ: to be unlike.
defer: to put off or delay.
    The two dresses will *differ* only in color.
    Do not *defer* today's debts to tomorrow.

TRANSCRIPTION POINTER

Spell out numbers when they represent ages:
    We want a boy who is at least eight years of age.

In a series of numbers, separate the numbers with commas:
    We hired these new employees in 1961, 1962, and 1963.

When two numbers form one item, spell out the smaller number:
    You ordered three 16-page booklets.

1

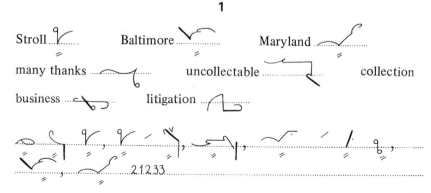

Stroll   Baltimore   Maryland

many thanks   uncollectable   collection

business   litigation

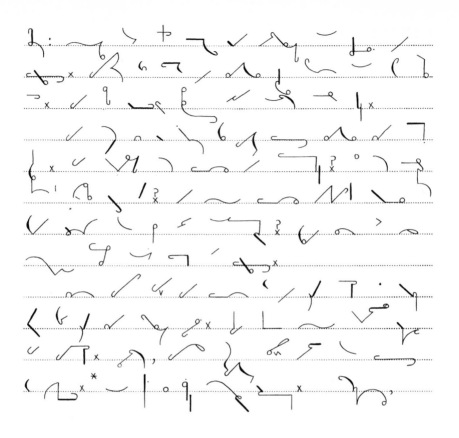

* Litigation refers to solving a dispute in court, according to law.

2

directly ⌇⌇⌇ to your company ⌇⌇⌇ surplus ⌇⌇⌇

investors ⌇⌇⌇

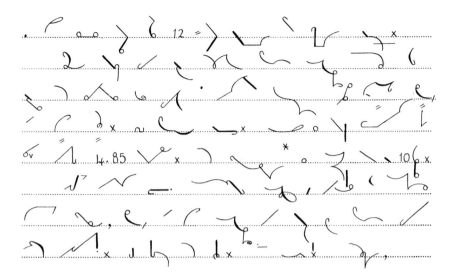

* Note spelling of *principal*.

3

computing ⟍   Social ⤳   Security ⟋

Internal ⌣   Revenue ⋏

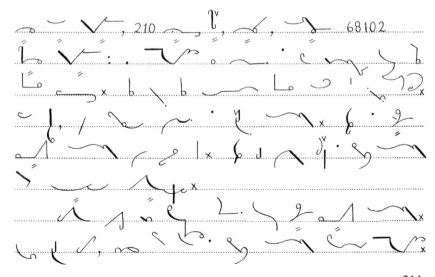

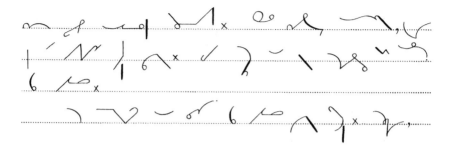

* A Social Security number is assigned to persons who are employed. Contributions to Social Security entitle you to old-age benefits.

CHALLENGE LETTER

UNIT 4

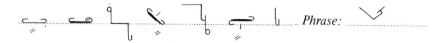 *Phrase:*

Key

Cliff gloves constructive Bluff activities Grove tough. *Phrase:* part of the

SPECIAL OUTLINES

break/brake

break: to separate into parts.

brake: (*noun*) an instrument for stopping motion.

(*verb*) to use the instrument to stop.

Can you *break* the piece of candy into three pieces?

Apply the *brakes* when you want the car to stop. If you *brake* it slowly, there will be a smoother stop.

TRANSCRIPTION POINTER

Do not use commas in a serial number, page number, address, etc.:

order No. 12357

Page 1231

7584 Willow Drive

In business correspondence, write the amounts of money in figures:

$10

$10.50

Repeat the dollar sign in a series of numbers:

We have cars for $3,000, $3,500, and $4,000.

Write indefinite amounts of numbers in words and specific amounts in numbers:

We have a few hundred dollars. You owe us $200.

1

Annapolis ⌇ factoring ⌇ financing arrangements ⌇

businessmen ⌇ inquire ⌇

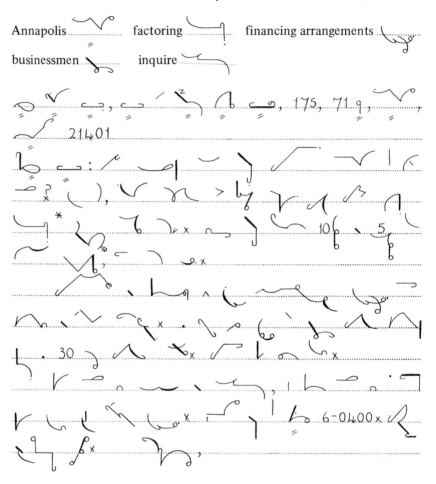

175, 71.9,

214.01

10.6, 5.

30

6-04.00 x

* What is *factoring*?

2

Bryant ⌇ transact ⌇ those who cannot ⌇

proxy ⌇ anticipated ⌇ renominated ⌇

1165, 214.01

* What is a proxy?

3

slowdown ... capital ... ill will ...

215

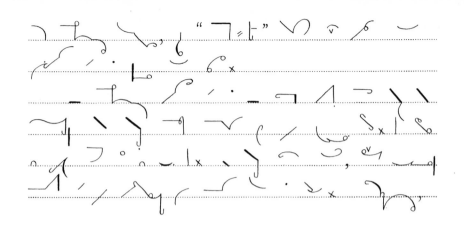

CHALLENGE LETTER

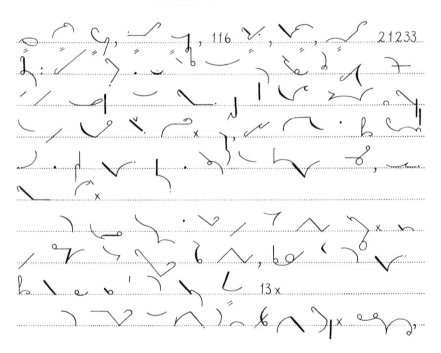

UNIT 5

VOCABULARY BUILDER

Key

divide division active positive selective prefer David motives
Phrase: type of

SPECIAL OUTLINES

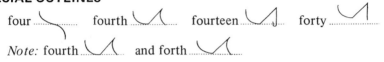

four .... fourth .... fourteen .... forty ....

Note: fourth .... and forth ....

TRANSCRIPTION POINTER

Write the word *number* as *No.* before a figure:

We have your order No. 647.

Do not write the decimal point unless there are cents:
$10 *but* $10.43

When the amounts are all under a dollar, use the sign for cents:
The price is 38¢ for this and 56¢ for that.

With mixed amounts, use the dollar sign and decimal point for cents standing alone:

We paid $6 for meat, $4.50 for canned food, and $.75 for coffee.

1

Peoria .... your corporation .... Burton ....

Almac .... synthetic ....

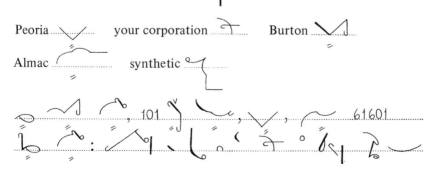

.... , 101 .... , ... , ... 61601 ....

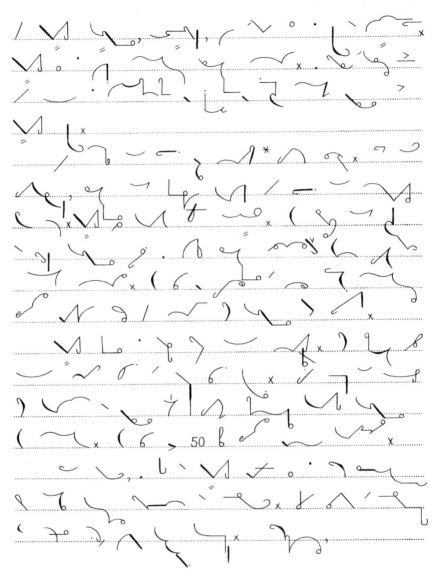

* What is a merger?

2

Rockford 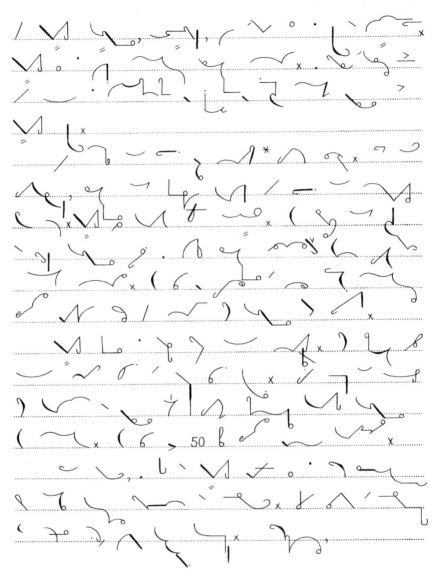 that you should consider

charge account installment rotating

* What is the meaning of "C.O.D."?

CHALLENGE LETTER

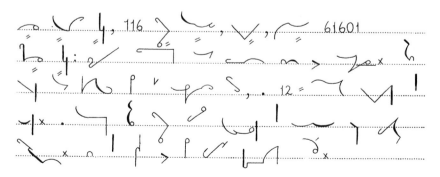

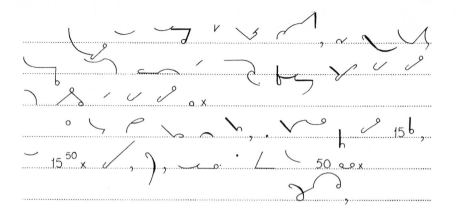

12 Entertainment

UNIT 1

VOCABULARY BUILDER

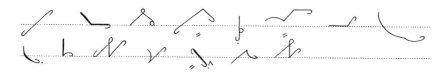

Key

winter begin response European outstanding American current afternoon evening demand western eastern Browning refund restaurant

SPECIAL OUTLINES

audience ⌐ℐ⌐   dance ℐ

TRANSCRIPTION POINTER

Names of days or months should not be abbreviated.

Use numerals for the day of the month when it follows the name of the month:

February 6, 19..   August 11, 19..

Words or numerals may be used when the date precedes the names of the month:

the sixth of June   the 20th of October

Express the date in words if the month is not named:

We will meet in Paris on the tenth.

1

Olympia 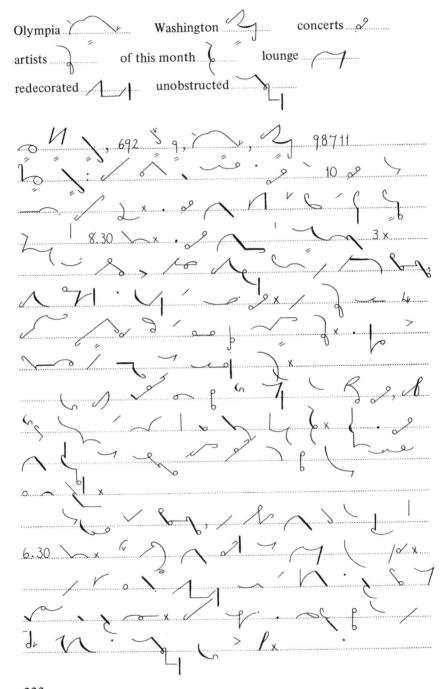 Washington concerts

artists of this month lounge

redecorated unobstructed

692 9, 9.8.7.11

10

8.30 3 x

6.30

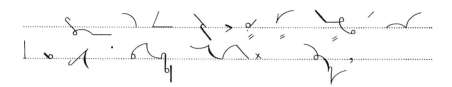

2

Associates 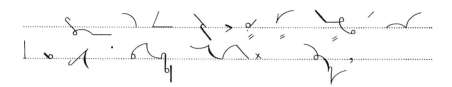   Seattle   musical

scheduled   festival   we are confident

98.135

UNIT 2

VOCABULARY BUILDER

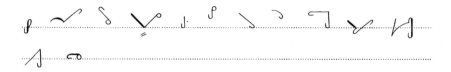

Key

student modern plans Burns tent stand open around curtain between children routine grounds

SPECIAL OUTLINES

often .... even ....

TRANSCRIPTION POINTER

In order to type the date of a letter so that it ends at the right margin, you must pivot for the date from the right marginal stop. Do this on the first of each month and set a tabular stop at the point on the scale which you reach. For the remainder of the month, tabulate to that point to type the date. On the tenth of the month, reset the tabular key one space to the left. This is a great time saver.

1

Montana .... Helena .... participating ....

courses .... Carpenter .... commitments ....

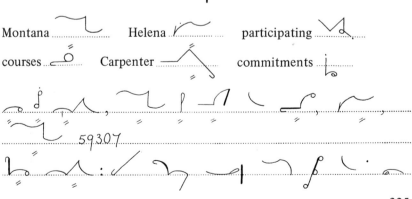

59307

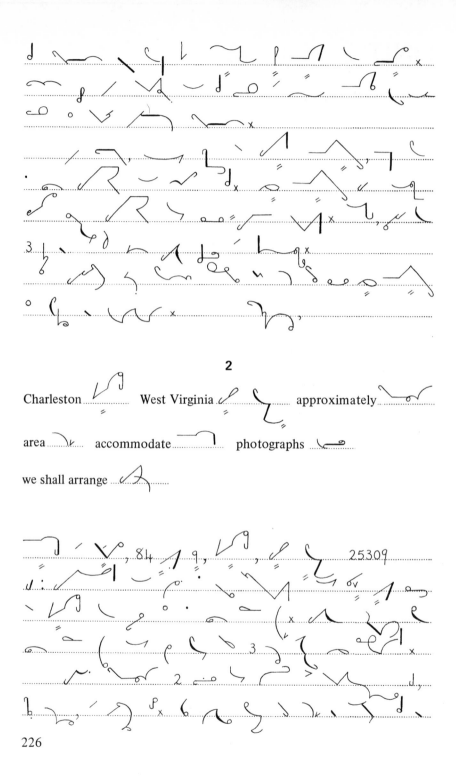

2

Charleston West Virginia approximately

area accommodate photographs

we shall arrange

, 84 , 9 , , 25309

, 3 , 2

226

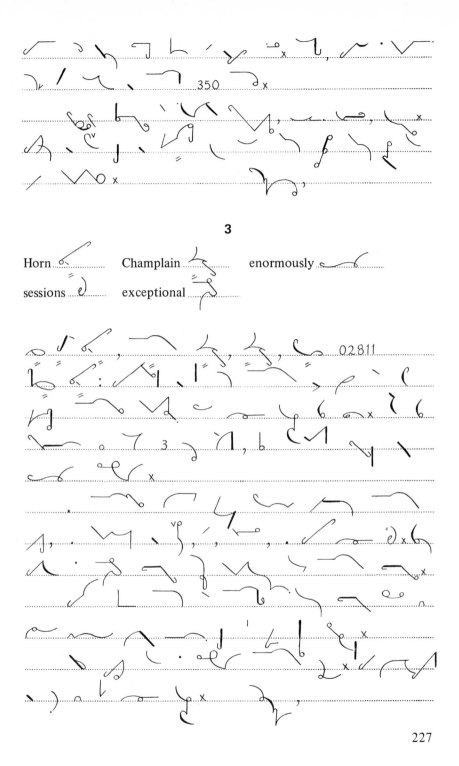

3

Horn　　　　　　Champlain　　　　　　enormously

sessions　　　　　exceptional

UNIT 3

VOCABULARY BUILDER

Key

painting beginning non-members obtain acceptance Tribune

SPECIAL OUTLINES

remainder............ reminder............

Downtown............ out of town............

TRANSCRIPTION POINTER

The abbreviations for a.m. and p.m. may be typed in lowercase letters. It is unnecessary to space between the letters:

5:30 p.m.
9:15 a.m.
six p.m.

1

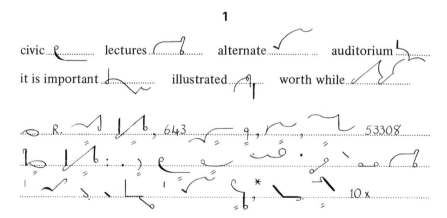

civic............ lectures............ alternate............ auditorium............

it is important............ illustrated............ worth while............

* What is meant by *alternate Fridays*?

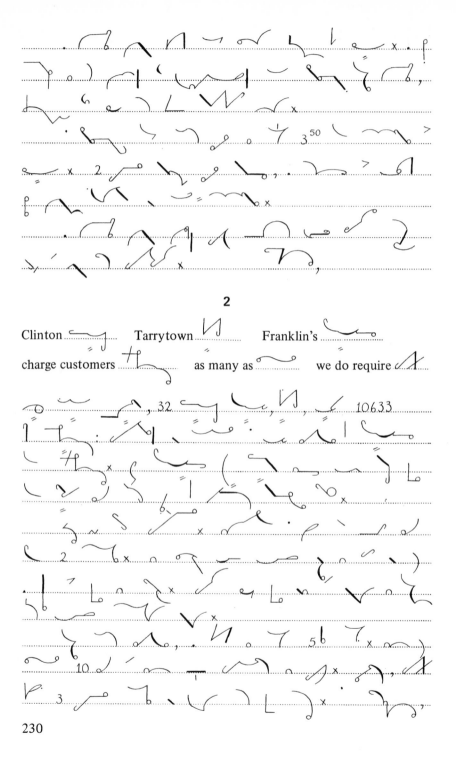

2

Clinton   Tarrytown   Franklin's

charge customers   as many as   we do require

32   10633

230

3

Professional 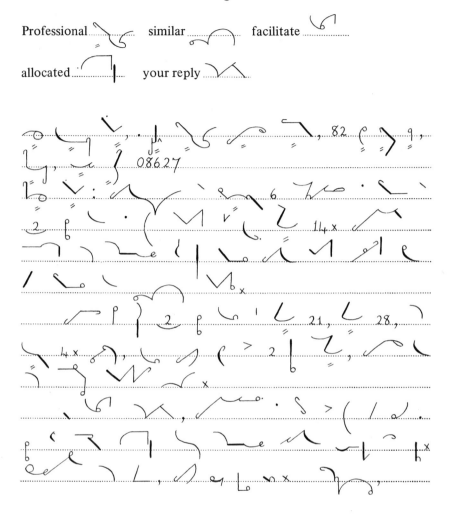 similar .... facilitate ....

allocated .... your reply ....

CHALLENGE LETTER

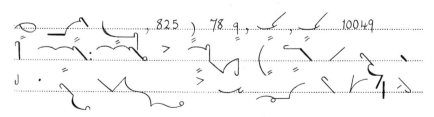

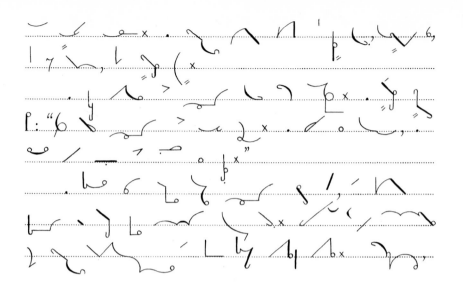

UNIT 4

VOCABULARY BUILDER

Key

events documentary screen spent consequently Chapin

SPECIAL OUTLINES

adapt ⎣...... adopt ⎣......

adapt means to make suitable; to adjust or to fit.
adopt means to take by choice.

We hope you can *adapt* these machines to our new requirements.
The government refused to *adopt* such punitive measures.

TRANSCRIPTION POINTER

In typewriting, correct fingering is an aid to both speed and accuracy. If you vary your fingering, you impede your own skill development.

When you are transcribing, all your attention should be given to the content of the material you are typing, and not to the mechanical elements of the skill.

1

Lyons............ whether you .... library ....

decade............ century .... negative ....

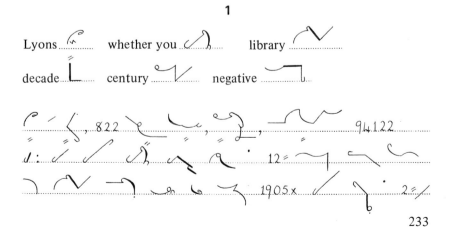

233

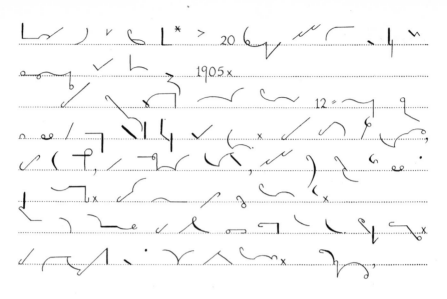

* What period of time is covered by (*a*) a decade (*b*) a century?

2

research department 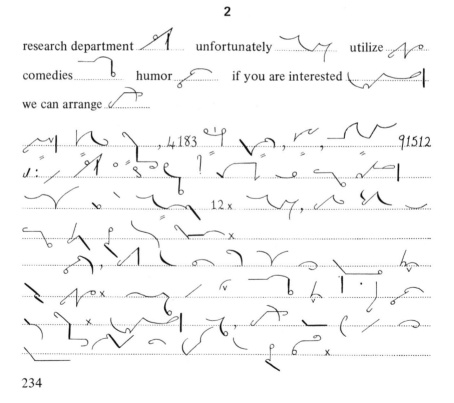 unfortunately ⁓⁓ utilize

comedies humor if you are interested

we can arrange

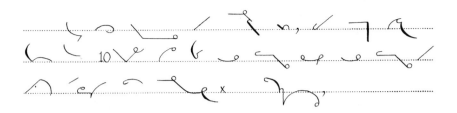

3

elsewhere 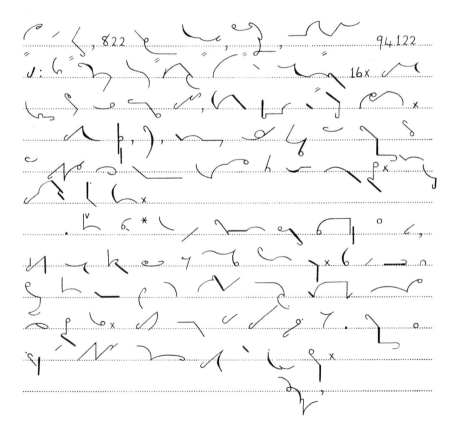 in order to .... films ....

that it will not be ....

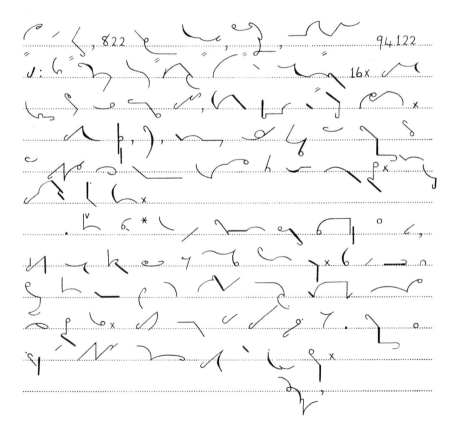

---

* A *time slot* in the television industry is the time scheduled for a show.

CHALLENGE LETTER

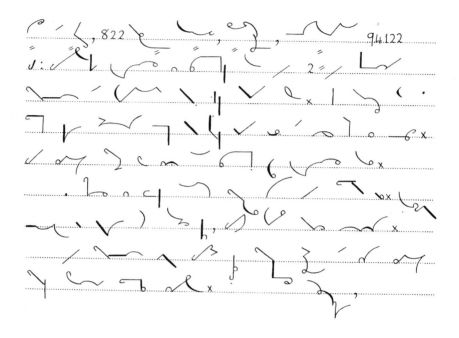

UNIT 5

VOCABULARY BUILDER

Key

client second again experience extend Dan million *Phrases:* it has been
we have done

SPECIAL OUTLINES

weather ⟋⟍   whether ⟍⟍

weather (*noun*) condition of the air with respect to heat, cold, rain.
whether (*conjunction*) if it be true; either.

    The *weather* report indicates that it will be fair today.
    We do not know *whether* the shipment arrived.

TRANSCRIPTION POINTER

    When you take dictation in an office, your employer may give you
enclosures to accompany the letters he has dictated. Mark the enclosures
lightly in pencil to indicate with which letters they are to go. Do *not* rely
on your memory!

    If you receive special instructions, these should also be written in your
shorthand notebook so that there will be no doubt or question about what
you were instructed to do. Keep a permanent record of instructions in a
special notebook to which you can refer when a similar job arises.

1

Hamilton   booked   type of   agency

newest   orchestra

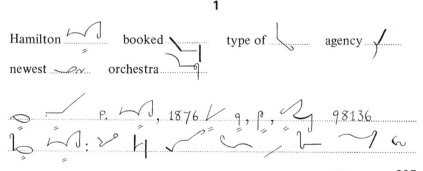

237

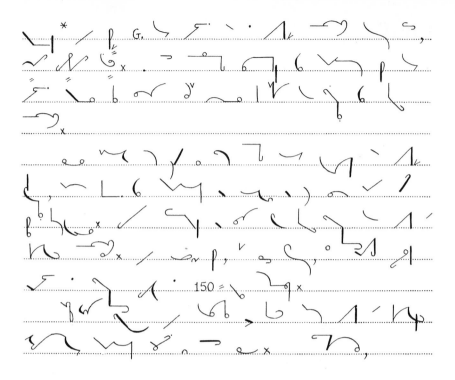

* What is the meaning of *booked*?

2

episodes 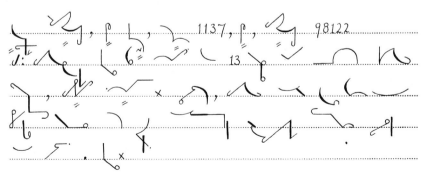 shipping department .... telecast ......

other companies .... courtesy ....

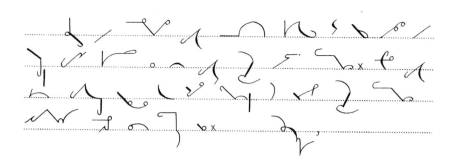

3

Theatrical .... Garcia .... discs .... facilities ....

specialize .... distributors .... jockies ....

G. .... , ... , 827 .... 46.9 ., ... ,

.... 10048 ....

13 Hobbies

UNIT 1

VOCABULARY BUILDER

Phrase:

Key

illustrations selection examination mission collection nation international attention sessions *Phrase:* in addition

SPECIAL OUTLINES

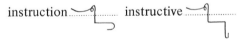

instruction   instructive

instruction (noun) knowledge or discipline, a lesson, an order.
instructive (adjective) serving to instruct or inform.
   The *instructions* were not clear and we lost our way.
   His demonstration was *instructive* and we knew just what to do.

TRANSCRIPTION POINTER

   Always make use of the fractions which appear on the typewriter keyboard whenever possible. However, if the material you are typing contains fractions which are not on the keyboard, they should be created by using the slant sign between numbers. Be consistent in your typing. Do not use the fractions which appear on the keyboard when you are typing others which do not appear on the keyboard in the same piece of copy:

Keyboard fractions: ½ ¼

Other fractions: 7/8 4/5 2/6 1/4

1

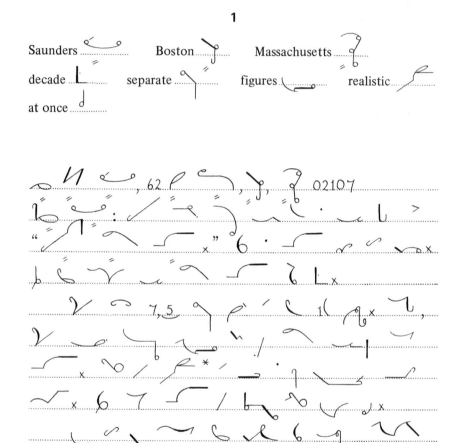

Saunders   Boston   Massachusetts

decade   separate   figures   realistic

at once

* What is meant by the expression "prices are realistic"?

Bridges 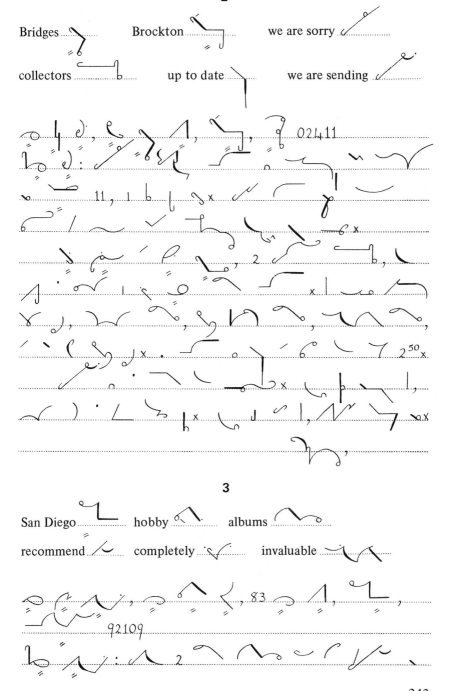 Brockton we are sorry

collectors up to date we are sending

3

San Diego hobby albums

recommend completely invaluable

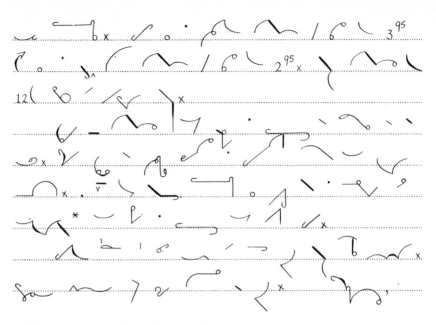

* What is the meaning of *invaluable*?

CHALLENGE LETTER

UNIT 2

VOCABULARY BUILDER

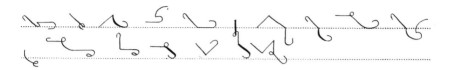

Key

perfection possession revision occasionally precaution distribution repetition provision expansion professional physician classifications attractions exhibition operation participation

SPECIAL OUTLINES

almost............ all most ....

We are *almost* ready.

We are *all most* anxious to attend.

TRANSCRIPTION POINTER

When typing whole numbers with fractions which are on the keyboard, do not space between the whole number and the fraction:

2½ 6¼ 15½

When typing whole numbers with fractions which are not on the keyboard, leave one space between the whole number and the fraction:

4 3/4 25 7/8

1

Printers............ Raleigh .... North Carolina ....

Managing............ Editor ....

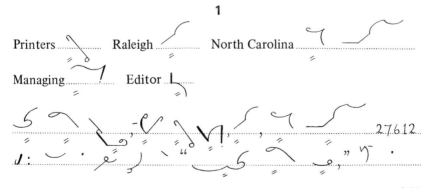

2.7.6.12.

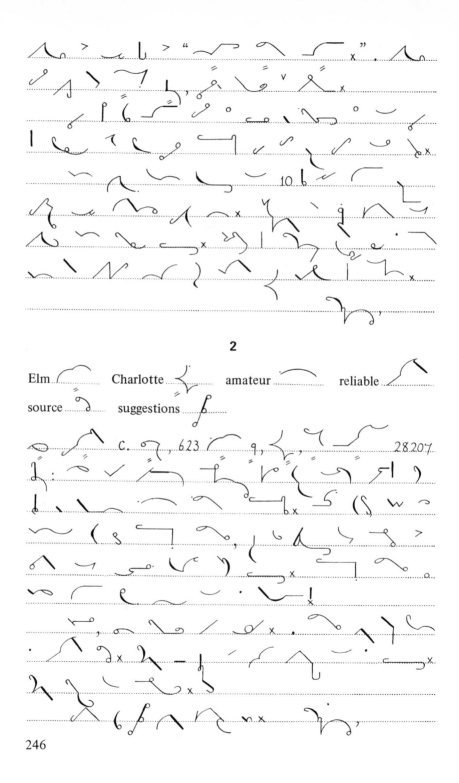

2

Elm ⌒ Charlotte ⋋ amateur ⌒ reliable ⌒

source ⌒ suggestions ♭

c. ⌒, 6.23 ⌒ 9, ⋋, ⌒ 28.20.7

Greensboro 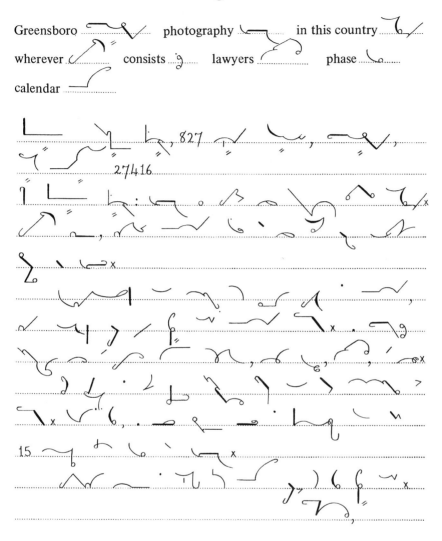 photography in this country

wherever consists lawyers phase

calendar

827

27416

15

CHALLENGE LETTER

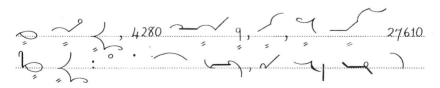

4280 27610

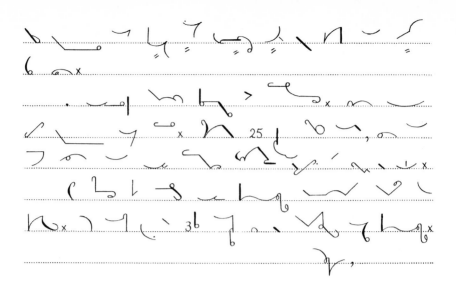

UNIT 3

VOCABULARY BUILDER

Key

fashion session motion association transportation admission
Phrases: in connection with in connection with the

SPECIAL OUTLINES

canvas .... canvass ....

canvas (*noun*) a heavy fabric used for tents and sails.
canvass (*verb*) to go to persons to ask for votes or orders.
    Our new sailboat has white *canvas* sails.
    The candidate will *canvass* the people in his district in order to get
more support.

TRANSCRIPTION POINTER

    The most direct method of centering a line is through the use of the
backspacing technique. Align your carriage so the the printing point
coincides with the center of the paper. Then backspace once for every
two letters or spaces in the line to be centered.

    A well-centered title on typewritten copy improves the appearance of the
page.

1

Arnold .... Mayhew .... secretary ....

procedures .... disposal ....

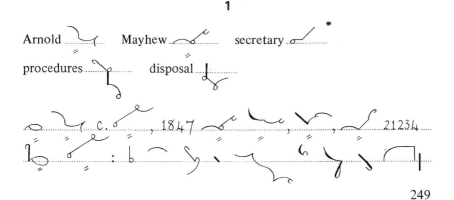

2

outing ⌐ Amateur ⌐ Guild ⌐ clubhouse ⌐

popular ⌐ activity ⌐ preliminary ⌐

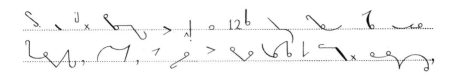

3

Revere  along with the techniques

participate announcement

251

CHALLENGE LETTER

UNIT 4

VOCABULARY BUILDER

Key

applications registration supervision additional *Phrase:* application form

SPECIAL OUTLINES

      course ⌐—ᵒ   coarse ⌐—ᵒ   cross ⌐—ᵒ

course (*noun*) direction; progress in time.

coarse (*adjective*) common; made up of large particles; rough.

    He will learn more in the *course* of time.

    This *coarse* fabric is not suitable for a girl's dress.

    If you *cross* the river, you can see its *course* better.

TRANSCRIPTION POINTER

You will become familiar with frequently-used proper names because of the practice you get in writing them.

However, this familiarity should alert you to the need for checking the spelling of names at all times. For example, names like *Johnson, Johnston, Jonson, Jansen,* and *Johnstown* can be confused very easily!

Such errors must be avoided; they can be very costly to your employer.

1

O'Rourke ⌐—   Adult ⌐   library ⌐   edit ⌐l

splice ⌐   your own ⌐   enroll ⌐

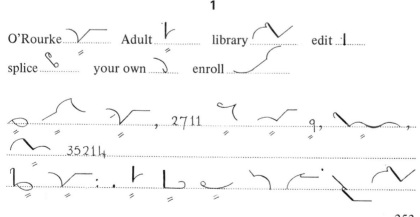

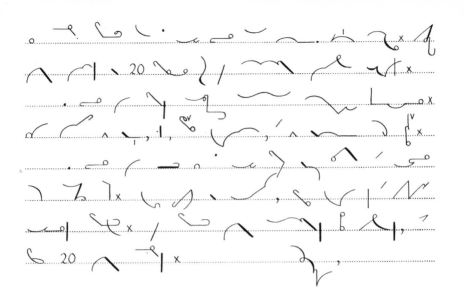

2

Rockland 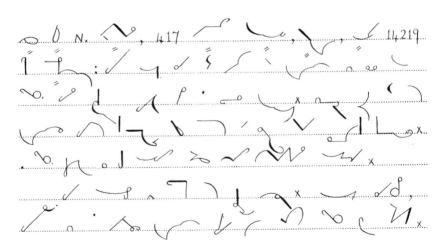   Buffalo   processing

laboratories   disappointment   sequence

exposure

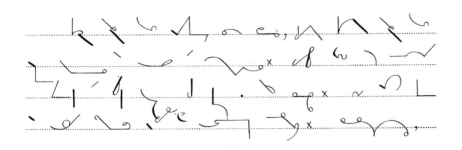

3

Luzon 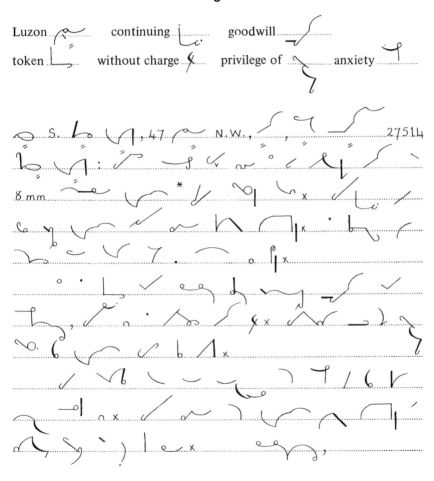continuing   goodwill

token   without charge   privilege of   anxiety

S.   ,47   N.W.,   27514

8 mm

---

* What is the meaning of *8mm. film*?

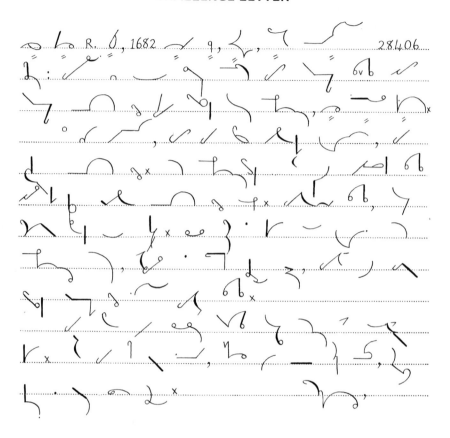

R. O., 1682 ... 28406

UNIT 5

VOCABULARY BUILDER

(shorthand outline)

Key

solution contribution intentions cooperation relations

SPECIAL OUTLINES

bases *(outline)*   basis *(outline)*

bases (*noun*) foundations; supports (plural of *base*).
basis (*noun*) component; fundamental principle.

The *bases* of the statues are stone.
On what *basis* would you question his right to vote?

TRANSCRIPTION POINTER

Even the expert occasionally writes a poor outline under the stress of fast dictation. When this happens, don't fret over it. Instead, when you hear an unfamiliar word, try to write something in shorthand which will suggest the word to you when you go over your notes after the dictation has ended.

Try not to miss the rest of the dictation because of difficulty over one unfamiliar word. You can generally find a substitute for a missing word or read one that is poorly written if you have the rest of the dictation and understand the content. As soon as possible, you should check the dictionary to learn the correct outline.

1

Wagner *(outline)*   Roosevelt *(outline)*   assistant *(outline)*   essentials *(outline)*

attendance *(outline)*   in our community *(outline)*   endeavor *(outline)*

essence *(outline)*

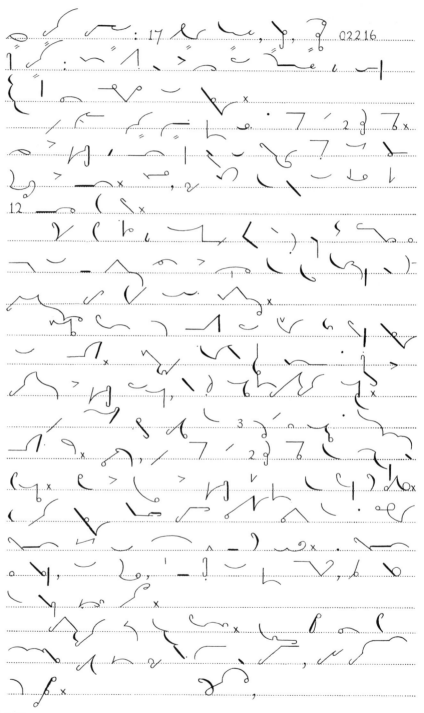

2

Zimmerman 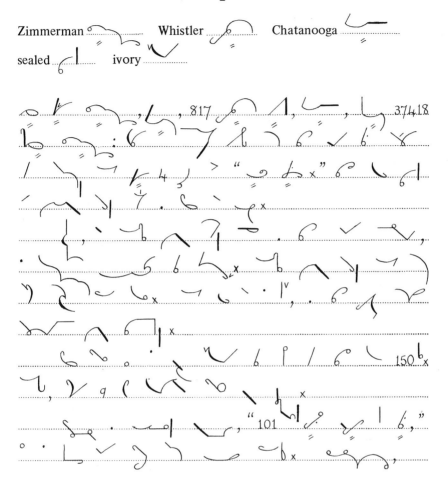 Whistler Chatanooga

sealed ivory

CHALLENGE LETTER

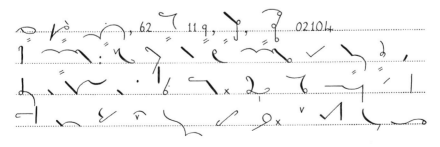

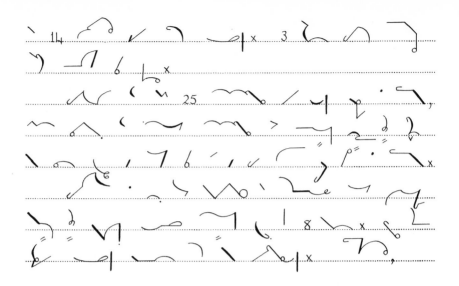

14 Law

UNIT 1

VOCABULARY BUILDER

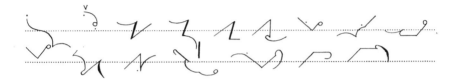

Key

confirm arising injury injured reject retainer parents military inquiries appearance herewith retail preference impartial reaction recover

SPECIAL OUTLINES

series _____ serious _____

series (*noun*) a number of things or events in succeeding order.
serious (*adjective*) earnest, important, solemn.

TRANSCRIPTION POINTER

The typing of numbers and special characters becomes more important once you are on the job than it appears to be while you are still a student. Numbers and special characters are used in typing dates, amounts of money, specifications, order and bill numbers, ZIP code numbers, and many other things in business papers.

Accuracy is of prime importance when typing numbers. At the same time, though, if you slow down to type numbers and special characters, you will not produce enough work to please your employer.

Daily practice can help you to improve your skill in typing numbers and special characters.

1

Lafayette  New Orleans Louisiana

Valdes coverage client pending

Maurice 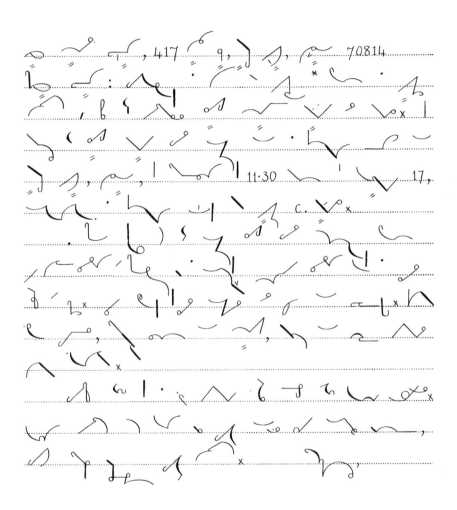   La Salle   Baton Rouge

Sergeant   collision   Richard

hospital   critical condition

* A retainer is a fee paid for engaging the services of a lawyer.

Lamport............ Universal .... Connors.............

dated............ summons .... Superintendent ....

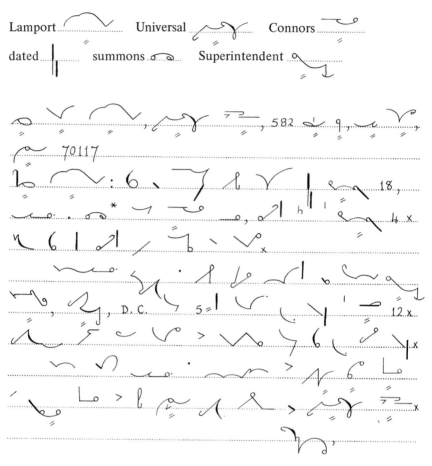

.... 70117 ....

.... 5.82 .... 18 ....

.... 4 x ....

.... D.C. .... 5 = ... 12 x ....

.... x ....

* A summons is an official notice to appear in court to answer charges.

CHALLENGE LETTER

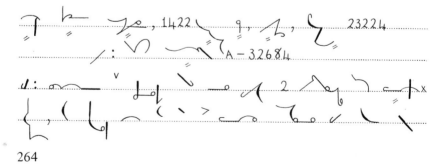

.... 14.22 .... 23.22.4 ....

.... A – 3.26.84 ....

.... 2 .... x ....

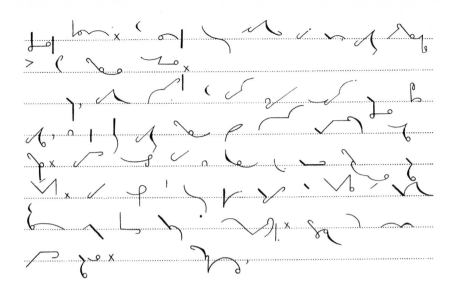

UNIT 2

VOCABULARY BUILDER

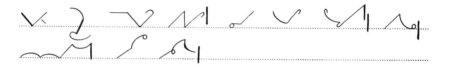

Key

borough original cooperation returned secretary foreign forwarded refused memoranda release resolved

TRANSCRIPTION POINTER

Type numbers of specifications in bills and orders exactly as dictated. Here are some examples:

Order No. 438
Style P57
Salescheck No. 32-1168
Purchase Order No. 482-7

1

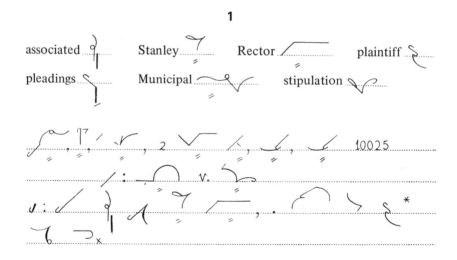

associated   Stanley   Rector   plaintiff

pleadings   Municipal   stipulation

10025

* The plaintiff is the complaining part in a suit.

266

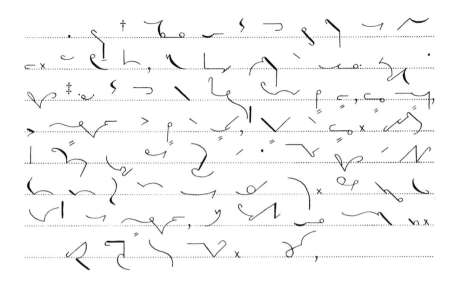

† The pleadings are the statements which set forth the plaintiff's claims.

‡ A stipulation is an agreement between attorneys concerning certain facts.

2

McCormack

notary public

defendant

transcript

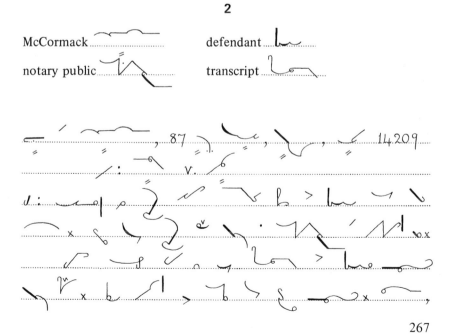

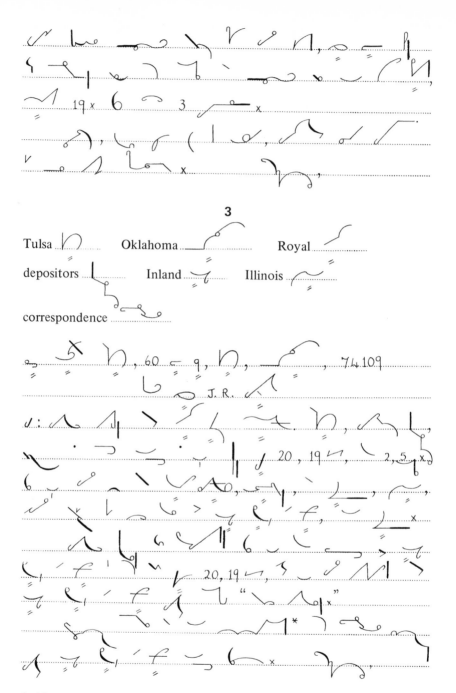

3

Tulsa   Oklahoma   Royal

depositors   Inland   Illinois

correspondence

J. R.

* *Memoranda* is the plural of *memorandum*.

268

CHALLENGE LETTER

UNIT 3

VOCABULARY BUILDER

Key

restriction sports anywhere Europe relationship territory working failure

SPECIAL OUTLINES

inquire .... acquire .... require ....

inquire means to ask or to investigate.

acquire means to get or to gain.

require means to need, to command, or to compel.

You may not *inquire* about lost articles today.

I hope that we can *acquire* this piece of property.

Do you *require* more help to complete the job?

TRANSCRIPTION POINTER

In law offices many documents are typed on legal paper which is 8½ in. X 13 in. in size and is ruled vertically at both the left and the right margins. The typing is done within the margins and is generally double spaced. Wills, acknowledgments, and affidavits, however, are often single spaced.

Printed forms are also used in lieu of completely typed documents. These contain blank spaces in which the details are filled in. When filling in information on printed forms, the typist must align the filled-in data with the printed lines.

1

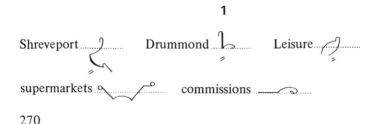

Shreveport .... Drummond .... Leisure ....

supermarkets .... commissions ....

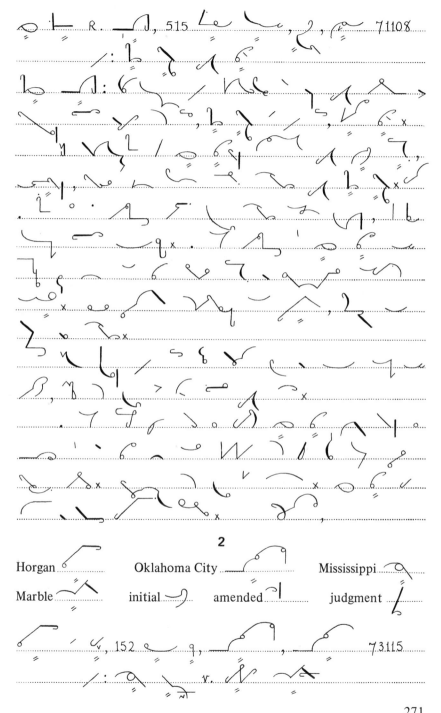

2

Horgan   Oklahoma City   Mississippi

Marble   initial   amended   judgment

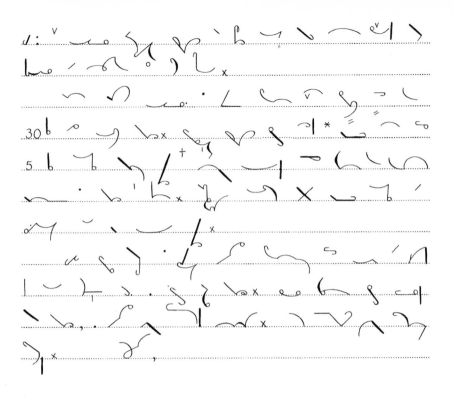

* *Amend* means to change, alter, or correct.
† Judgment: decree or sentence of a court.

CHALLENGE LETTER

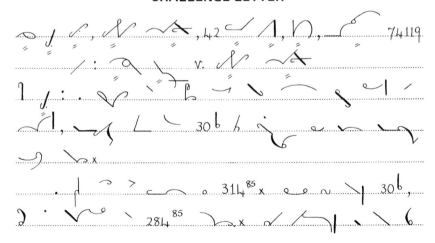

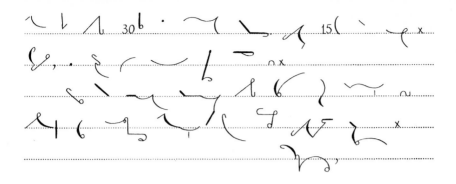

UNIT 4

VOCABULARY BUILDER

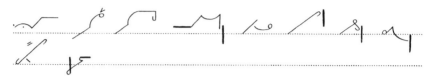

Key

America realize reluctant guaranteed recognize rendered responded
certified worn disregard

SPECIAL OUTLINES

regard-ed .... record-ed ....

to, too ....

TRANSCRIPTION POINTER

Many legal documents are bound at the top. To provide for this, a
margin of about 1¾″ should be left at the top of each page.

Pages following the first page should be numbered about 1″ from the
bottom edge of each page.

A few lines of typing should appear on the last page of a document so
that the signature lines do not appear on a page by themselves. A solid
underscore is used for signature lines. These are started one or two spaces
to the right of the center of the page and extend almost to the right margin.
If the document is to be witnessed, signature lines for witnesses are typed
on the left-hand side of the page.

1

Levore .... Martinez .... Santiago .... Chile ....
acceptable .... in the arrangements ....

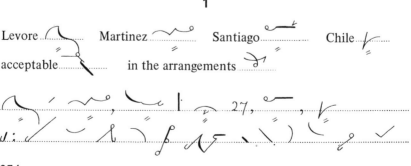

2

Phoenix ⌣......ₒ...   graciously ↗......   later than ....⌒.........

institute ...⌐ſ.........

* What is the meaning of *responded in kind*?

CHALLENGE LETTER

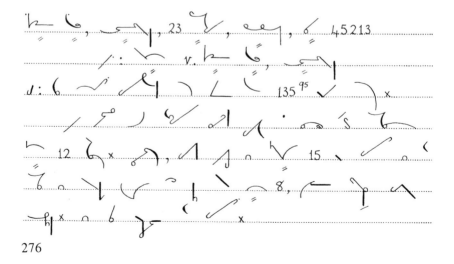

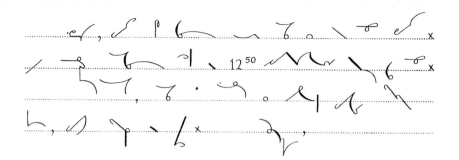

UNIT 5

VOCABULARY BUILDER

Key

conferences appear route concerned carrier forth power earliest

SPECIAL OUTLINES

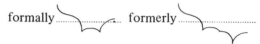

formally   formerly

formally (*adverb*) with regard to convention or cermony; stiff.
formerly (*adverb*) heretofore; with regard to time past.

TRANSCRIPTION POINTER

Accuracy is especially important when typing legal documents. Major corrections and erasures must be initialed by the principal parties. Most law firms do not permit any erasures in the typing of wills.

When you realize that these documents may become the subject of court action, you will understand why such high standards are enforced.

1

Elizabeth   Macon   probate   estate

handwriting   that the matter requires

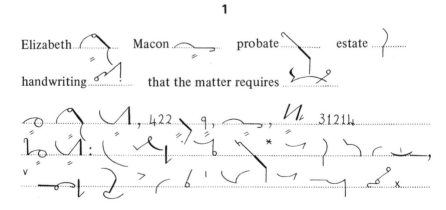

* *Probate* is the official proof of the last will and testament of a deceased person.

278

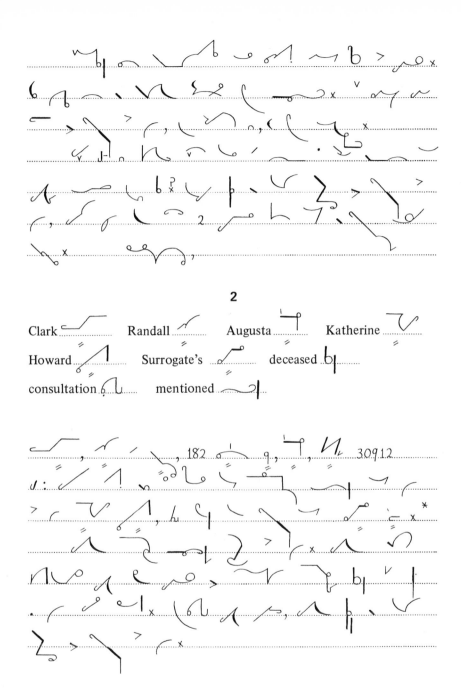

2

Clark ⎯ Randall ⎯ Augusta ⎯ Katherine ⎯

Howard ⎯ Surrogate's ⎯ deceased ⎯

consultation ⎯ mentioned ⎯

, 182 , , , 30912

* A Surrogate's Court deals with the disposition of property of persons who have died.

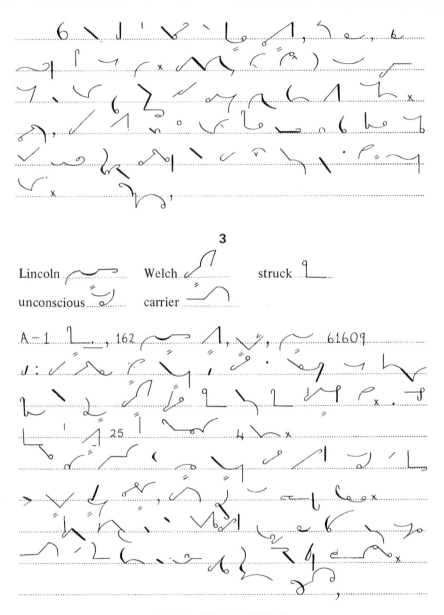

3

Lincoln ⌒⌐ Welch ⟋ struck ꟼ

unconscious ⟋ carrier ⌒⌐

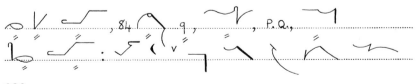

CHALLENGE LETTER

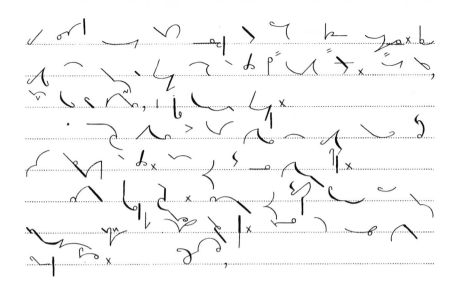

15 Shipping

UNIT 1

VOCABULARY BUILDER

Key

Mohawk hundredweight hence adhere happens Omaha harbor Hamilton

SPECIAL OUTLINES

Compare the outline for hope .⌒......
with *hope* as written in phrases: *we hope* ..⌒.... *I hope you will* ...⌣....

TRANSCRIPTION POINTER

Postscripts are afterthoughts. They are indented five spaces from the margin of the letter and are typed a double space below the initials (or whatever is the last line under the initials). The postscript starts with the letters P.S. For example:

IK:YD
Enc.

P.S. We are still awaiting word regarding your order for the Christmas season.

282

1

Juneau 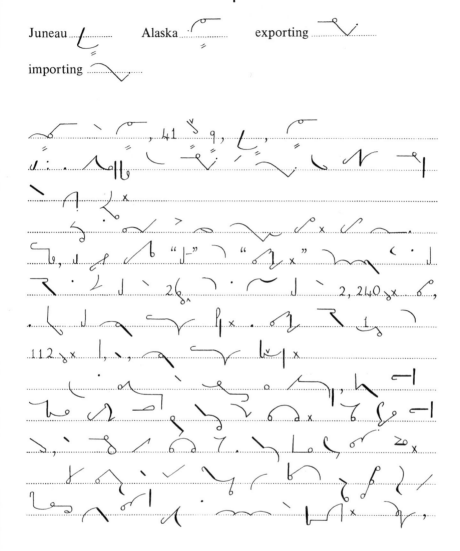 Alaska exporting

importing

2

F.O.B.   inland   extra charges

minimum requirement   marine insurance

* F.O.B. means Free on Board and refers to the point of delivery.

3

Swedish 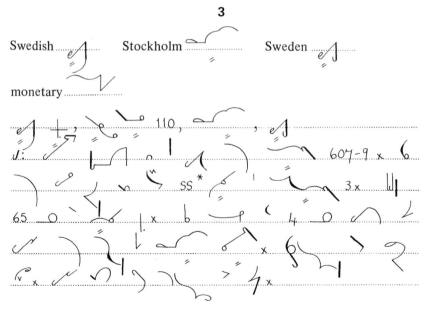 Stockholm

Sweden

monetary

* SS is the abbreviation for steamship.

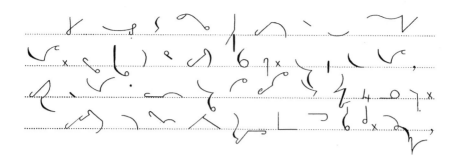

CHALLENGE LETTER

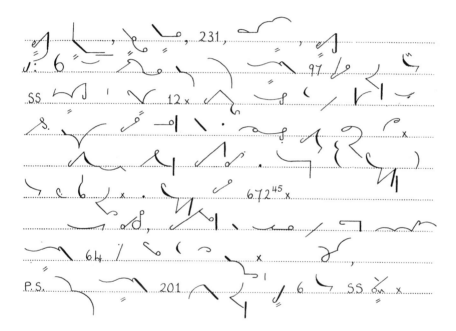

UNIT 2

VOCABULARY BUILDER

Key

Hall Household Hume hurried holiday hesitate harmonious happy
hard hurt

SPECIAL OUTLINES

herewith   herein   hereby

herewith means with this.
herein means in or into this.
hereby means by means of this.

TRANSCRIPTION POINTER

Express percentages in figures with the words *per cent* written out as
two words. The per cent sign may be used with percentages which occur
very frequently, as in accounting material. For example:

We received 15 per cent of the amount due.
Our statistics show the following sales: coats 40%; suits 20%;
hats 30%; shoes 10%.

1

St. Paul   Minnesota   Capetown

vessel   alternative

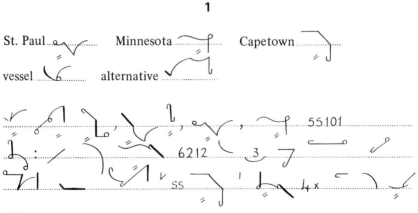

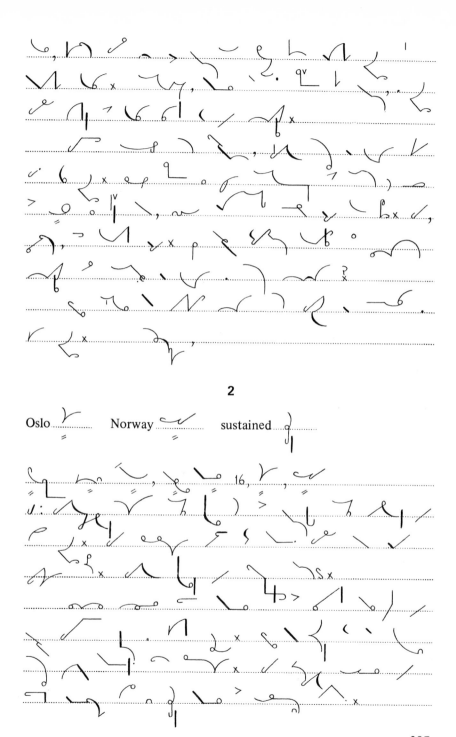

2

Oslo ⟨shorthand⟩ Norway ⟨shorthand⟩ sustained ⟨shorthand⟩

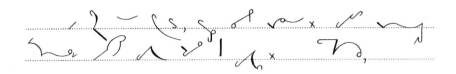

3

Jorge 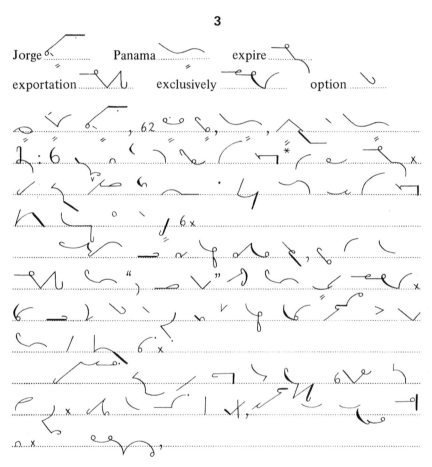 Panama .... expire ....

exportation .... exclusively .... option ....

* A letter of credit is a letter addressed by a banker to his correspondents certifying that the person named can draw up to a specified sum.

CHALLENGE LETTER

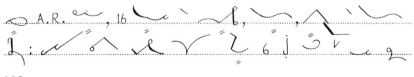

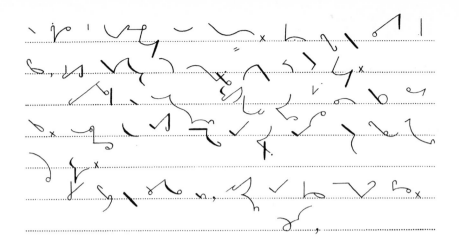

UNIT 3

VOCABULARY BUILDER

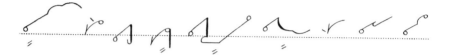

Key

Harlem holes hidden Hillside Headquarters Havana haul highway
highlights

SPECIAL OUTLINES

worth while/worth-while

Worth while should be written as two words. However, when used as
an adjective before a noun, the words are hyphenated. For example:

We believe it would be *worth while* to investigate the quotations.
It would be a *worth-while* venture.

TRANSCRIPTION POINTER

Ratios and proportions should all be written in figures:

The ratio of boys to girls was 2 to 1.
We see a 50-50 chance that your team will win the game.

1

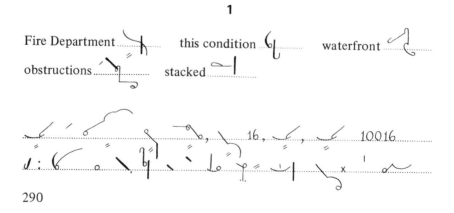

Fire Department   this condition   waterfront

obstructions   stacked

16,   10016

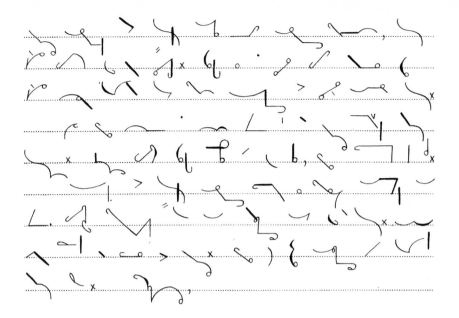

2

Minneapolis Hold-More ⌐⌐⌐ dead-weight

eliminated ⌐⌐⌐ competitive ⌐⌐⌐ carload ⌐⌐⌐

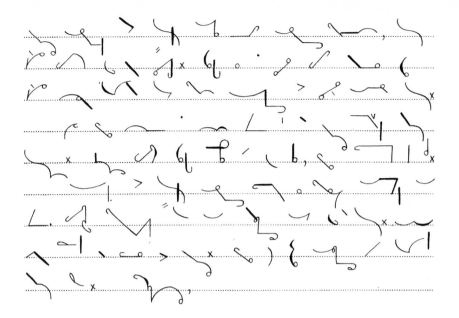

2

Minneapolis _____   Hold-More _____   dead-weight _____

eliminated _____   competitive _____   carload _____

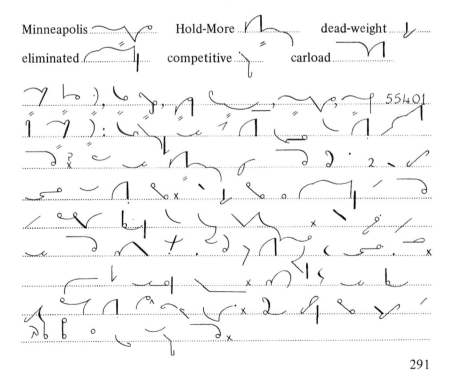

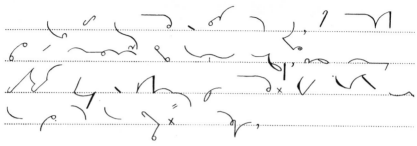

3

Salt Lake City Utah automatic

dependable

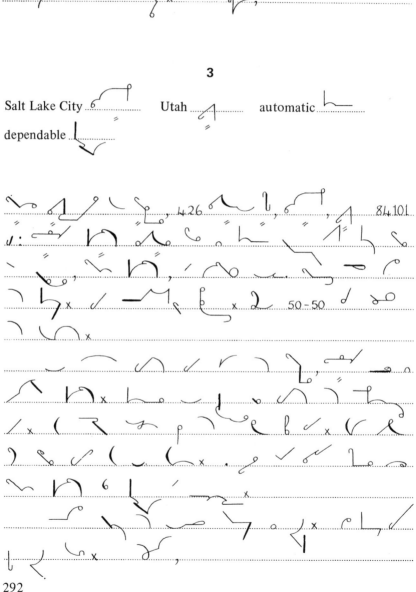

CHALLENGE LETTER

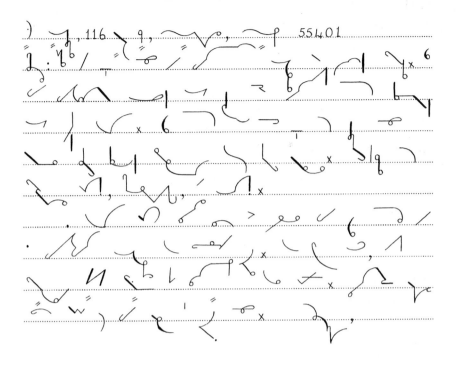

UNIT 4

VOCABULARY BUILDER

Key

Henry Houston heavy hardships helpful Hosiery

SPECIAL OUTLINES

may be/maybe

may be means might happen.

maybe means perhaps.

It *may be* coming on the tenth.

Maybe we will go with you.

TRANSCRIPTION POINTER

In business correspondence, numbers are used for weights, distances, and measures of all kinds:

The rug was 12 by 20 feet.

We drank 2 quarts of milk.

Your order was for two dresses, size 8.

We traveled 12 miles in the 85-degree heat.

1

Venezuela regulations government

contracts attachments temporary

impose

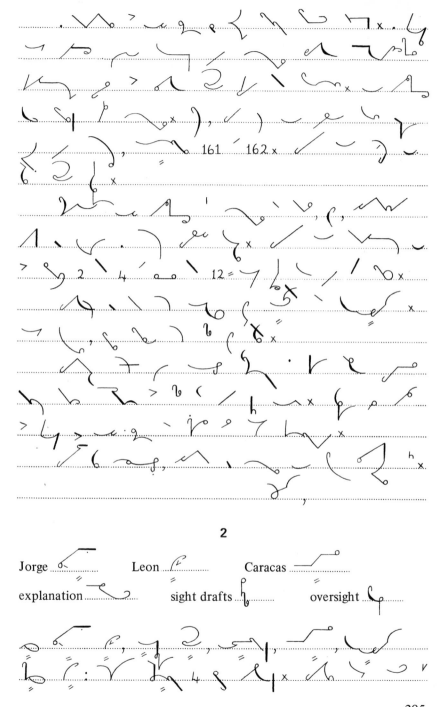

2

Jorge ⌒   Leon ℓ   Caracas ⌐°

explanation ⌐⌐   sight drafts ⟋   oversight �

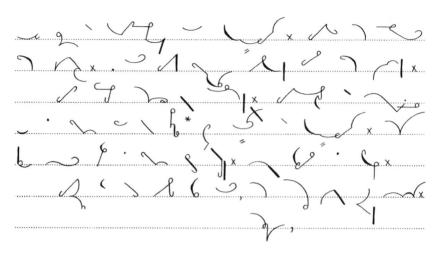

* A sight draft is a bill or draft which demands payment upon presentation.

CHALLENGE LETTER

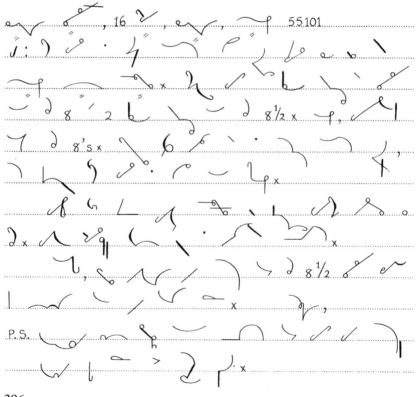

UNIT 5

VOCABULARY BUILDER

Key

history Herley Hygiene Harvey Hill

SPECIAL OUTLINES

enable ....⟍....   unable ....⟍....

enable means to make able or easy.

unable means not able.

Take the short way because it will *enable* you to arrive ten minutes earlier.

We are *unable* to attend the ceremony.

TRANSCRIPTION POINTER

When a weight consists of several words, the words should not be separated by commas:

We bought 2 pounds 6 ounces of meat.

Spell out time of day when used with *o'clock* but use numbers with *a.m.* or *p.m.*:

We left at ten o'clock.

I want to arrive at 10 a.m. for the meeting.

1

two hundred ....2.,.....   documents ....

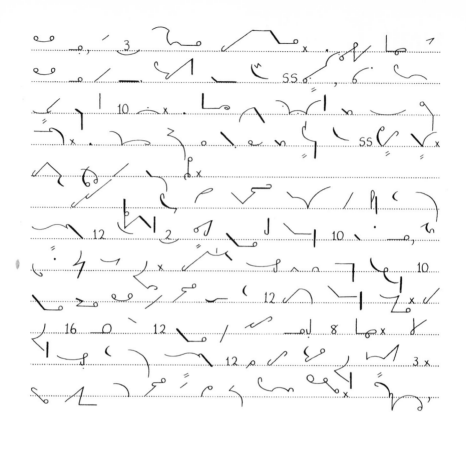

2

transportation charges 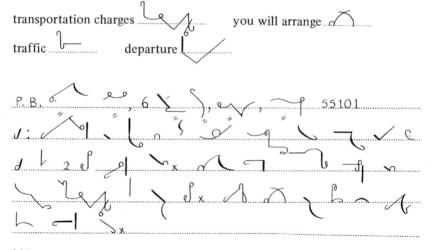 you will arrange

traffic   departure

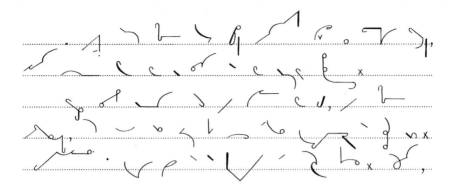

3

minimum charges   subscribed

their business

CHALLENGE LETTER

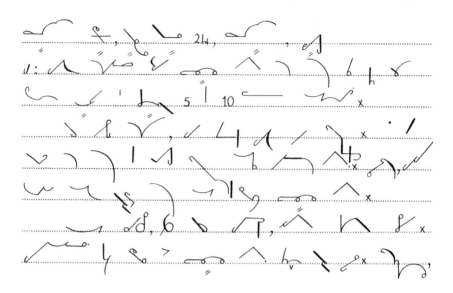

16 Insurance

UNIT 1

VOCABULARY BUILDER

Key

policyholder health absolutely overlooked continental facilitate
handling directly fault filing formal hospitalization until family
quarterly enrollment costly annually

SPECIAL OUTLINES

notify ⁀ɭ   inform ⁀ɭ

notify means to give notice of, to make known.
inform means to tell, to give information.

TRANSCRIPTION POINTER

The hyphen is easy to use in compound expressions like *up-to-date*
or *well-known* if you bear in mind these simple rules:

(*a*) When the expression which modifies the noun comes before the
noun, use the hyphens:

We want an up-to-date showroom.
This well-known refrigerator is very low in price.

(*b*) When the compound expression follows the noun, do not hyphenate:
This factory is not up to date.
This merchandise is low priced.

(*c*)   When the adjectives can be used independently, generally a hyphen is not used:

> Here is a stamped, addressed envelope.
> I need a four-foot shelf.

1

Constance 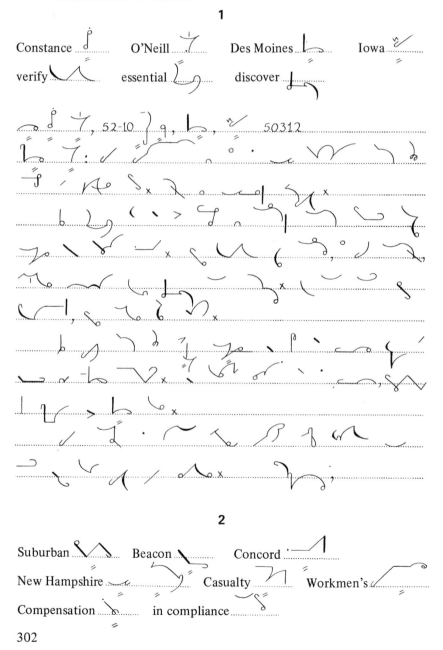 O'Neill   Des Moines   Iowa

verify   essential   discover

Suburban   Beacon   Concord

New Hampshire   Casualty   Workmen's

Compensation   in compliance

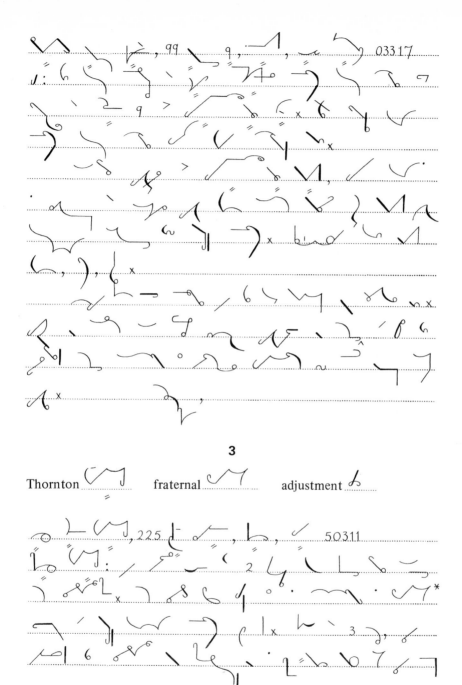

3

Thornton ⌒⌐⌐   fraternal ⌒⌐/   adjustment ♭

* What is the meaning of *fraternal*?

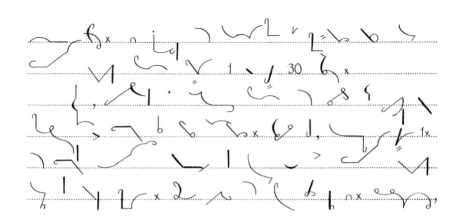

CHALLENGE LETTER

UNIT 2

VOCABULARY BUILDER

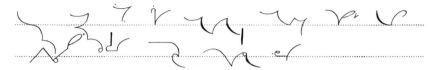

Key

fairer insurers annually control involved unfortunately earliest
evaluation reupholstering adequately careful impulsive consequently

SPECIAL OUTLINES

insure   ensure   assure

Insure and *ensure* mean to obtain insurance on or for. *Assure* was formerly
used in this sense, too, but now it is generally used to mean to give confidence
or to make certain.

TRANSCRIPTION POINTER

Do not hyphenate modifiers which precede the noun if the first one is an
adverb ending in *ly*:

    She is a poorly trained employee.
    This is a badly made coat.

When in doubt, consult an up-to-date dictionary. Usage changes and a
dictionary is your most reliable authority.

1

Fuller   Milwaukee   Wisconsin
arose   negotiating   optimistic   processing
reopen

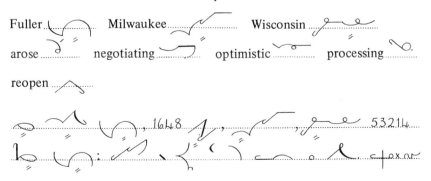

16448   53214

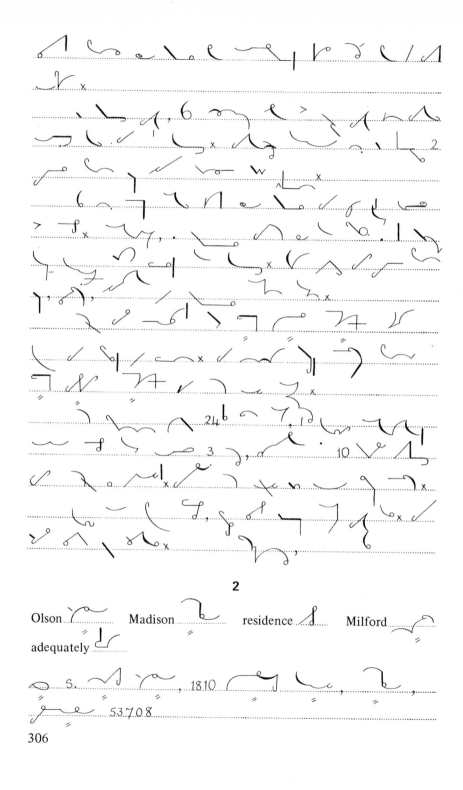

2

Olson ⌐ Madison ⌐ residence ⌐ Milford ⌐

adequately ⌐

⌐ S. ⌐ ⌐, 1810 ⌐ ⌐ ⌐,

⌐ ⌐ 53.7.0.8

CHALLENGE LETTER

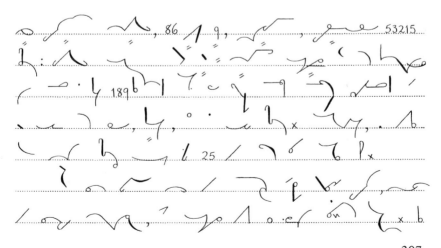

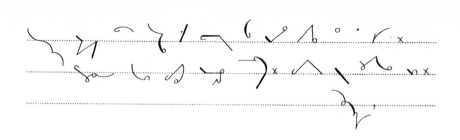

UNIT 3

VOCABULARY BUILDER

Key

leg whiplash involvement liability cancel apparently casual

SPECIAL OUTLINES

collect............⌐....   correct............⌐....

TRANSCRIPTION POINTER

Good judgment is needed in planning a letter of two or more pages. Here are some important things to remember:

Use letterhead stationery for the first page — plain sheets for the additional pages.

Use the same left and right margins for all pages of the letter.

Plan the typing so that at least one paragraph appears on the last page of the letter.

Whenever possible, begin each page with a new paragraph. NEVER divide the last word on a page.

Each page of the letter must be identified by means of a heading. Here is a practical style:

Mrs. John Jones   2   June 12, 19—
   (Addressee)

1

Investigators ....   physician ....   assured ....

nausea ....   diagnosed ....   accuracy ....

discretion ....

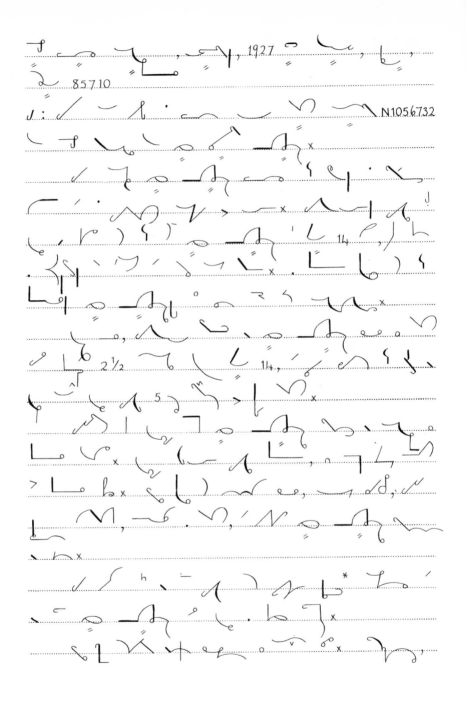

* What is the meaning of the phrase *act with discretion*?

Hayward 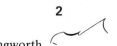 Longworth ⌢ remainder ⌐

ascertain

CHALLENGE LETTER

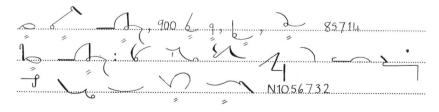

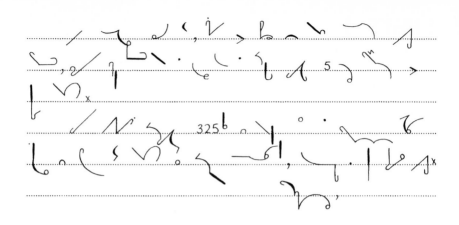

UNIT 4

VOCABULARY BUILDER

Key

alleged insurer failure ability accordingly reveals automobile rule liable professional

SPECIAL OUTLINES

courteous .... courtesy ....

courteous (*adjective*) polite, civil.

courtesy (*noun*) politeness or civility.

His *courteous* manner won him the affections of the ladies.

We were treated with the utmost *courtesy* at all times.

TRANSCRIPTION POINTER

These general rules should be followed in preparing a typewritten manuscript:

Type on one side of the paper only, as you do in typing letters; prepare at least one carbon copy.

If the first page has a title, leave a top margin of two inches. Center and capitalize the title.

Leave a top margin of one inch on the remaining pages.

If a manuscript is to be bound on the left, leave a left margin of $1\frac{1}{2}''$ and a right margin of $1''$.

1

Ronald .... occurrence .... subdivision ....

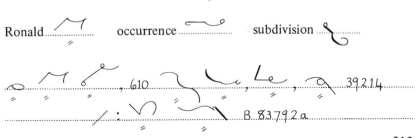

* *Allege*: to assert without proof but with implied readiness to prove.

2

Biloxi ... reconsider ... sustained ... breach ...

50 ... 39618

B 83792a

314

CHALLENGE LETTER

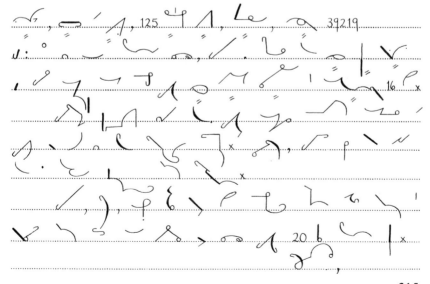

UNIT 5

Key

properly late merely older naturalization

SPECIAL OUTLINES

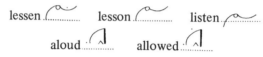

lessen .... lesson .... listen ....

aloud .... allowed ....

aloud means out loud, so as to be heard.

allowed means to permit, to grant or to assign.

TRANSCRIPTION POINTER

Manuscript copy is generally double spaced. A first draft may be triple spaced to provide room for corrections and changes in copy.

When the copy contains quoted material, it should be single spaced and indented at least five spaces from the left and right margins of the general copy. This is also true of tabulated inserts.

Each page of the manuscript should have approximately the same number of lines of typing, except for the first page.

1

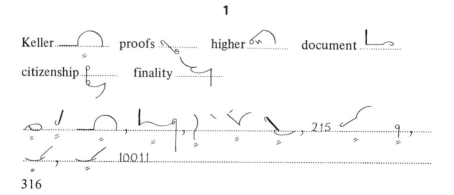

Keller .... proofs .... higher .... document ....

citizenship .... finality ....

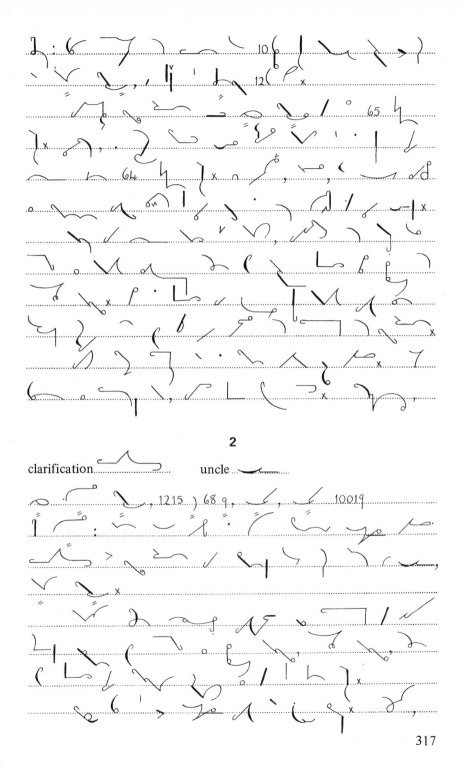

2

clarification............................ uncle.................

nephew .... beneficiary ....

900 *06117*

7824958

* A beneficiary is one who receives a gift or benefit.

CHALLENGE LETTER

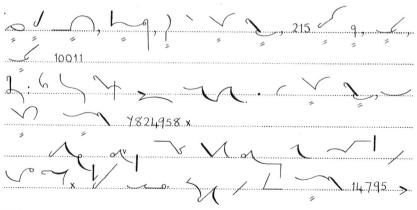

215 *10011*

7824958

147.95

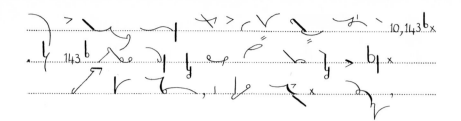

17 Machinery and Equipment

UNIT 1

VOCABULARY BUILDER

Key

Shine machine machinery shrewd Sheffield Fisher accomplished Shield sure surely

TRANSCRIPTION POINTER

The secretary should be familiar with different types of machines used in offices.

Duplicating machines are used for making multiple copies. Various types of duplicators are:

Stencil — Wax stencils are typed (or cut manually) and placed on machines using ink or paste.

Gelatin — Master copy is made and placed on a gelatin bed.

Liquid — Special carbon paper is used for the master, and duplication is through liquid in the machine.

Type-set — Type is set and covered by an ink ribbon.

Offset — A metal or paper master is transferred to a rubber mat.

Photocopiers — make an exact copy with paper sensitive to light.

1

Augusta ⌐ Maine ⌐ your inquiry ⌐

for your business ⌐ appropriate ⌐

P. B. ⌐ , 207 ⌐ 9 , ⌐ , ⌐ 04123

2

Bangor ⌐ offset ⌐ duplicator ⌐

eliminate ⌐

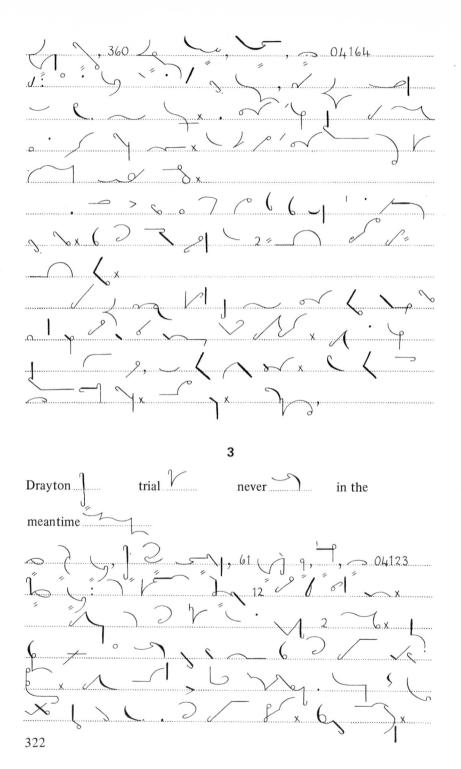

3

Drayton .... trial .... never .... in the

meantime ....

322

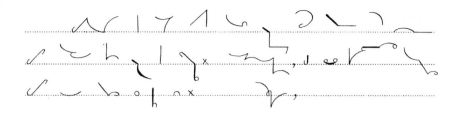

CHALLENGE LETTER

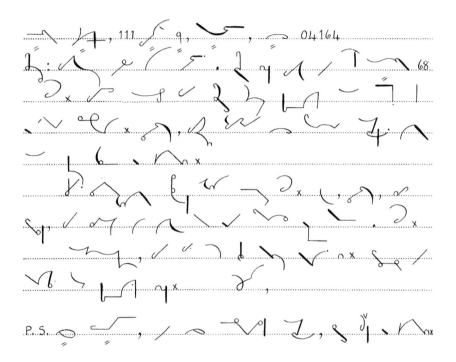

UNIT 2

VOCABULARY BUILDER

Key

Shadow Michigan assures push share

SPECIAL OUTLINES

danger-s  dangerous

TRANSCRIPTION POINTER

Adding machines and calculators have registers which record numbers to be computed. They can be used with a tape for listing (called a listing machine) or without a tape (called a nonlisting machine).

Among the listing machines are the ten-key and the full-keyboard.

Among the nonlisting machines are the key-driven and the crank-driven.

The adding machine will add, subtract, and multiply. The key-driven calculator is used mostly for adding and multiplying. The crank-driven is used when all four operations are required.

1

Columbus .... microfilm .... economy ....

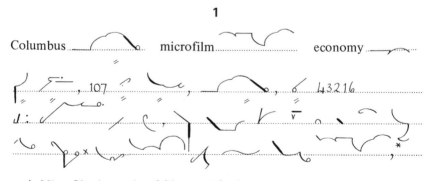

* Microfilm is a strip of film used for keeping a photographic record of reduced size of written or printed matter.

324

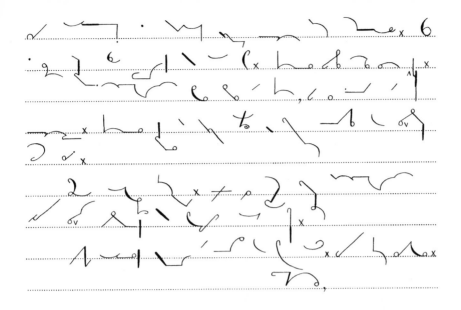

2

Cleveland ⌐⌐ overstitch ⌐ thread control ⌐

lubrication ⌐

44101

16

16

325

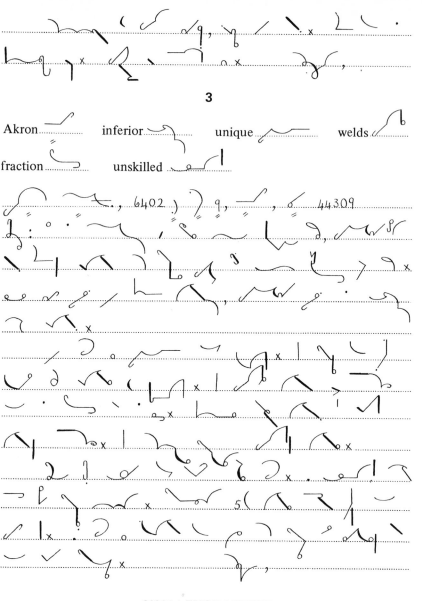

3

Akron

inferior

unique

welds

fraction

unskilled

CHALLENGE LETTER

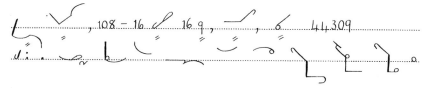

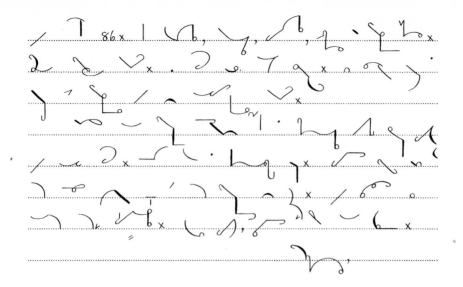

UNIT 3

VOCABULARY BUILDER

Key

Nash Shell Sugar shape Shirt Shale brush *Phrase:* shipping department

SPECIAL OUTLINES

there ..⟩.... there are ...⟩... there is ...⟩... they are ✓

TRANSCRIPTION POINTER

Dictation machines are used in many offices. Discs and belts are used to record the dictation. The belts are placed in the transcribing machines and are used by typists who listen to them and type. The plastic disc looks like a phonograph record. Some are used only once. Others may be erased or shaved and reused.

Wire and tape records are sometimes used with machines for dictation. These tapes are erased and used again for new dictation.

These machines have a function when an employer wants to dictate at a time when his secretary is not available, or if he wants to dictate while she is transcribing other more important or "rush" work.

1

Cheyenne .... Wyoming .... copier ....

simplicity .... nationwide ....

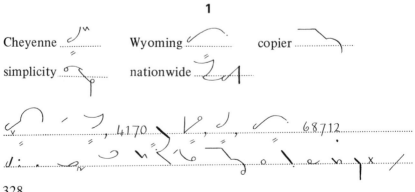

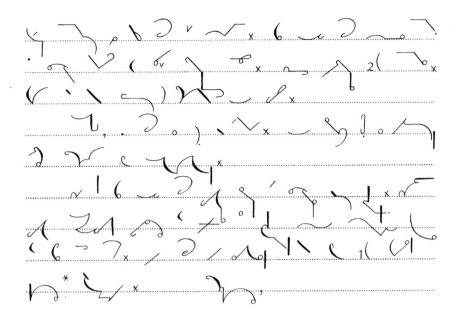

* What is meant by an *authorized dealer*?

2

old-fashioned 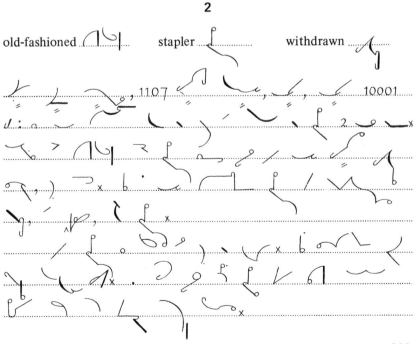 stapler   withdrawn

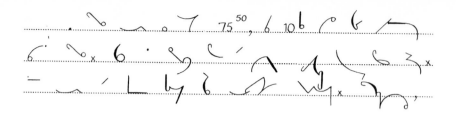

3

liquid 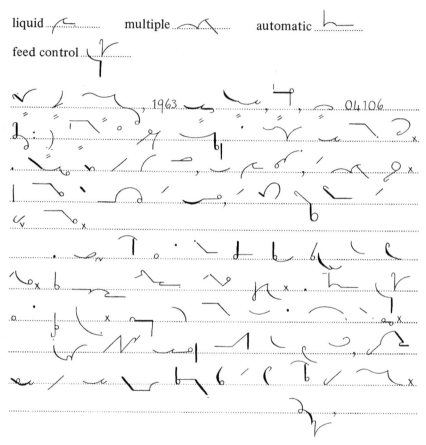 multiple .... automatic ....

feed control ....

1963 .... 04106 ....

CHALLENGE LETTER

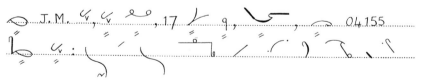

J.M. .... 17 .... 04155 ....

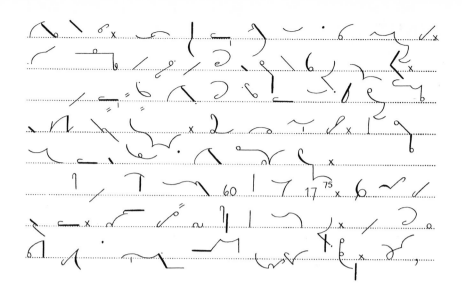

UNIT 4

VOCABULARY BUILDER

Key

Sheer Shaker brochure rush anxious Shanghai

SPECIAL OUTLINES

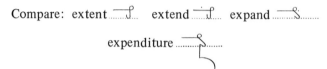

Compare: extent ⌐ʃ extend ⌐ʃ expand ⌐⸜

expenditure ⌐⸜

The *extent* of the damage is not known.
We hope you will *extend* every courtesy to him.
Do you think that we can *expand* our headquarters?
The *expenditure* involved was over one hundred dollars.

TRANSCRIPTION POINTER

The Varityper machine sets up typewritten matter for photocopy work. It looks like a regular typewriter and has a standard typewriter keyboard. As the name indicates, there are many sizes and kinds of type which can be set into the machine. The spacing between letters can be controlled as the size is adjustable.

The Automatic typewriter can retype the same letter over and over. It works from a master record. When the record is placed on the machine, the typewriter automatically types the letter.

1

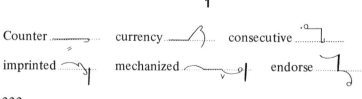

Counter _____ currency _____ consecutive _____

imprinted _____ mechanized _____ endorse _____

* What is a *mechanized file*?

typewriter ......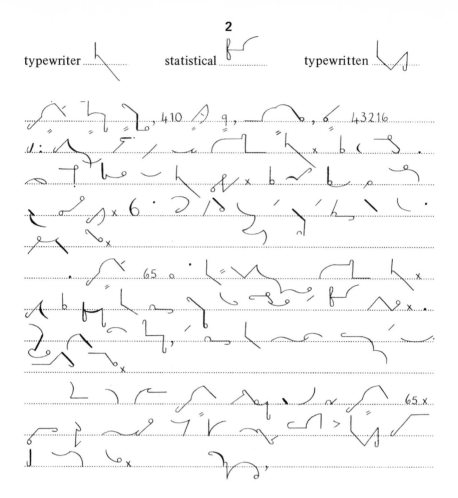...... statistical .... typewritten ....

2

CHALLENGE LETTER

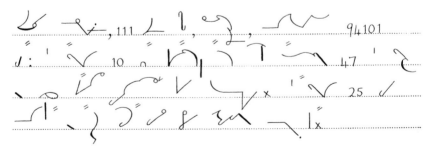

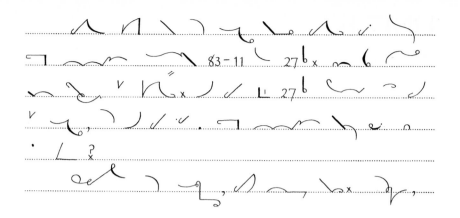

83 - 11 27 ᵇ x

27 ᵇ

?
x

UNIT 5

VOCABULARY BUILDER

Key

Danish Dash showing crash Lash

SPECIAL OUTLINES

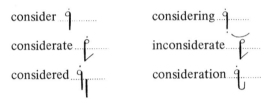

consider   considering

considerate   inconsiderate

considered   consideration

TRANSCRIPTION POINTER

    PBX boards may have cords (suitable for firms handling a large number of calls) or may be cordless. Incoming and outgoing calls are directed through the PBX boards. Calls coming in to a firm are answered by the switchboard operator who makes the connection with the party being called.

    Outgoing calls are either dialed directly by the person making the call or, in some cases, by the operator, who then connects the two parties.

1

pattern   cutter   fraction   garments

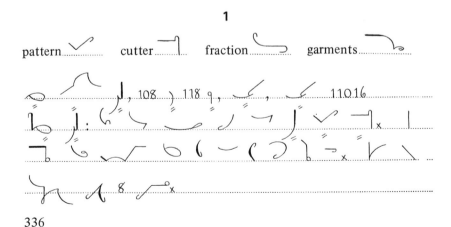

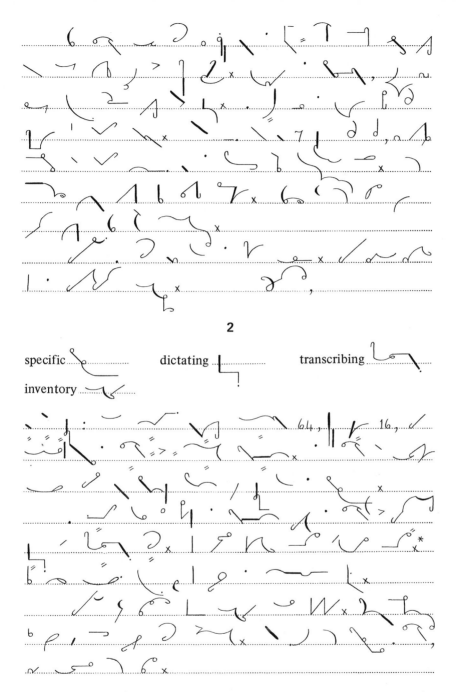

2

specific _____   dictating _____   transcribing _____

inventory _____

* How does a conference call differ from a regular telephone call?

Intercom .... switchboards ....

* An intercom is an interoffice telephone that allows executives to speak to each other or to any employee.

CHALLENGE LETTER

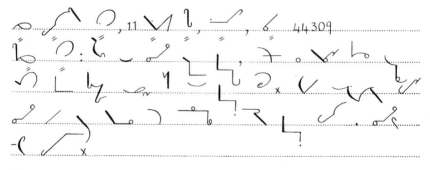

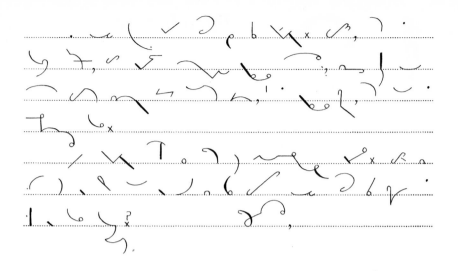

18

Real Estate

UNIT 1

VOCABULARY BUILDER

Key

forwarded otherwise between quick withdraw

SPECIAL OUTLINES

access .... excess ......Q.... accede .... exceed ......T....

access (*noun*) means or way of approach.
excess (*noun*) more than is required; great abundance.
accede (verb) to agree, assent; attain to an office.
exceed (verb) to be more or greater; surpass.

> Can he gain *access* to the room?
> On flights, one is charged for *excess* baggage.
> He is so persuasive, you will *accede* to his request.
> Production this year will *exceed* last year.

TRANSCRIPTION POINTER

> *Under separate cover* has the same meaning as *under another cover.*
> Letters which contain either of these phrases do not have enclosures.

340

1

Quinn 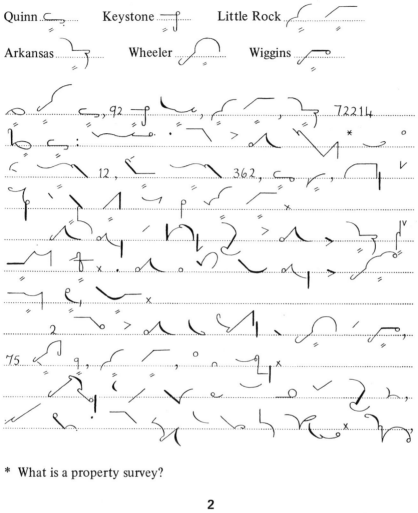 Keystone Little Rock

Arkansas Wheeler Wiggins

* What is a property survey?

2

Bismarck North Dakota adjournment

it is understood

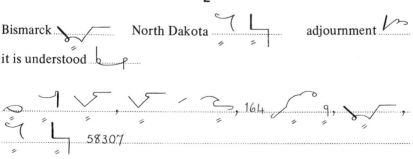

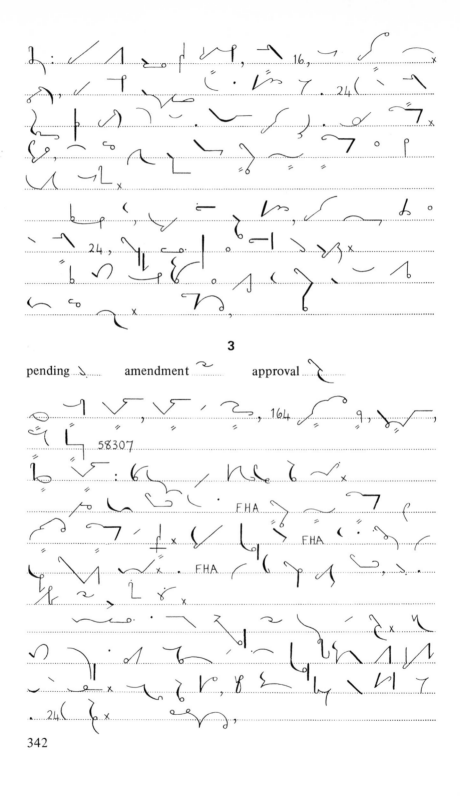

3

pending ‿‿‿ amendment ‿‿‿ approval ‿‿‿

164

58307

F.H.A.

F.H.A.

F.H.A.

24

CHALLENGE LETTER

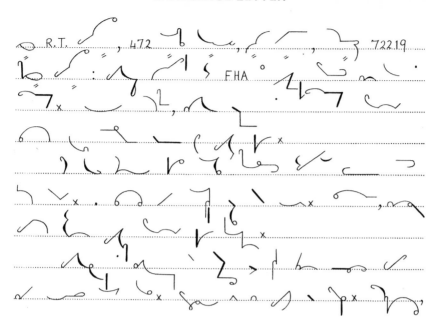

UNIT 2

VOCABULARY BUILDER

Key

square wiser elsewhere wife meanwhile questions require Ward Woods

SPECIAL OUTLINES

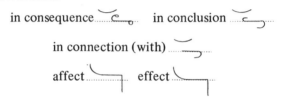

in consequence in conclusion

in connection (with)

affect effect

affect (*verb*) means to impress or influence; attack (as a disease).
effect (*noun*) means result or outcome.
effect (*verb*) to bring about a change.

How will the news of her failure *affect* him?
What will be the *effect* of the new legislation on our sales?
It will be difficult to *effect* the change at your first meeting.

TRANSCRIPTION POINTER

Accounts Payable is a term used in bookkeeping to mean the record of money owed for the purchase of goods or services.

This is a liability of the business.

1

Webster Wilshire Dayton

Franklin procure factors

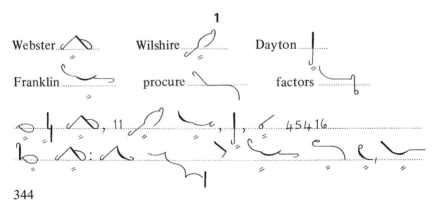

, 11 , , 45416

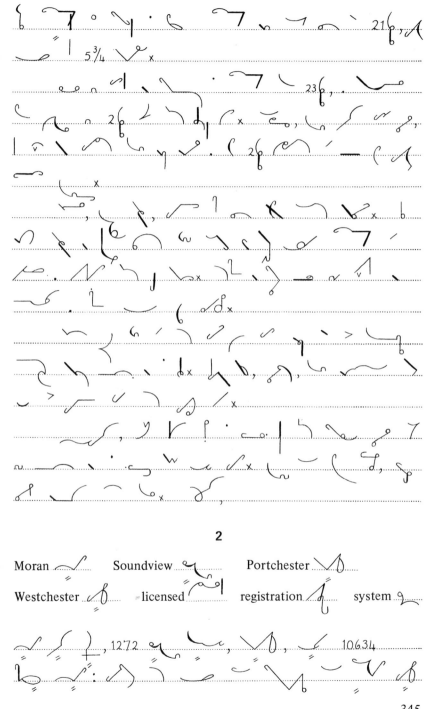

2

Moran ⟨shorthand⟩ Soundview ⟨shorthand⟩ Portchester ⟨shorthand⟩

Westchester ⟨shorthand⟩ licensed ⟨shorthand⟩ registration ⟨shorthand⟩ system ⟨shorthand⟩

⟨shorthand⟩ , 12.7.2 ⟨shorthand⟩ , ⟨shorthand⟩ , 10.6.34

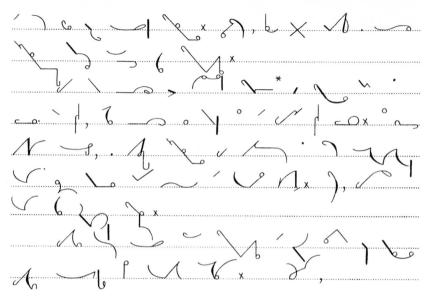

* What is a licensed broker?

CHALLENGE LETTER

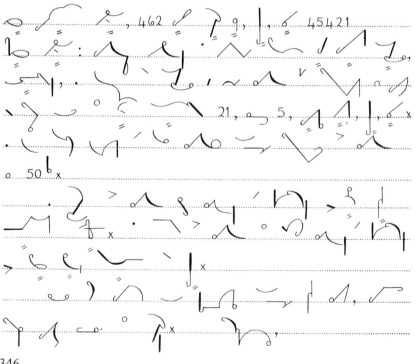

UNIT 3

VOCABULARY BUILDER

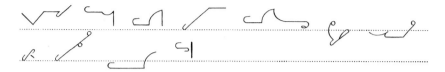

Key

parkway quantity quality work qualifications southwest inquiries won't warehouse quickly acquainted

SPECIAL OUTLINES

sight ⌄ᶜ   site ⌄ᶜ

sight (*noun*) a view, vision.
site (*noun*) location.

>   After an hour in the stalled car, the tow truck was a welcome *sight*.

>   This will be the *site* of the new museum.

TRANSCRIPTION POINTER

Accounts receivable represent money due from customers for purchases.

This is an asset of the business.

1

Montpelier ⌒   Vermont ⌒   heirs ⌒   listings ⌒

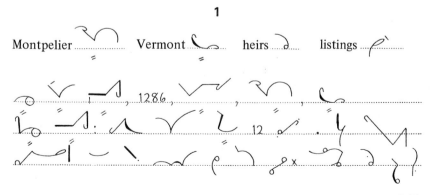

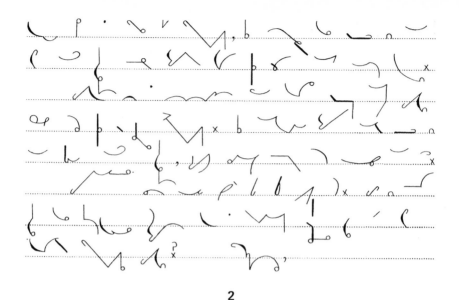

2

Leonard ⌒ Crescent ⌒ Elmsford ⌒

appraiser ⌒ congratulated ⌒

38 10507

18

R.

348

periodically 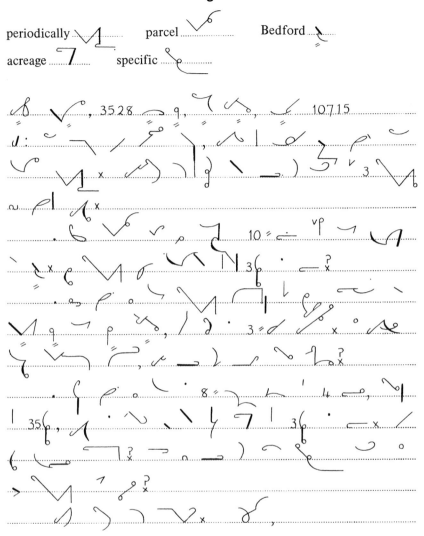   parcel   Bedford

acreage   specific

35.28   107.15

CHALLENGE LETTER

.68

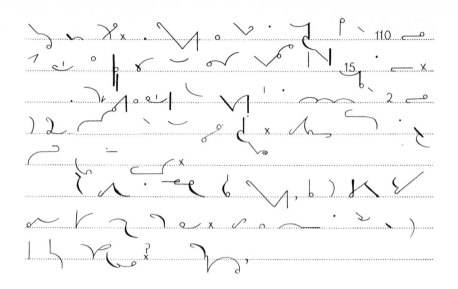

UNIT 4

VOCABULARY BUILDER

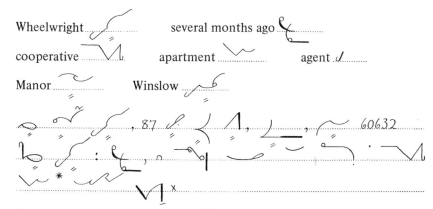

Key

welcome reservoir somewhat worn

SPECIAL OUTLINES

quality .... quantity ....

TRANSCRIPTION POINTER

Titles of position and honor are capitalized when used before personal names:

Government officials:	Mayor John Doe
	Ambassador John Smith
Executive positions:	Vice-president Thomas Black
Professional and Medical:	Dean Martha White
	Dr. George Green
Armed Services:	Col. R. T. Clay
	Lieut. Arthur May

1

Wheelwright .... several months ago ....

cooperative .... apartment .... agent ....

Manor .... Winslow ....

.... , 87 .... , ... , ... 60632 ....

.... : .... , ...

.... * .... x ....

* What is a cooperative apartment?

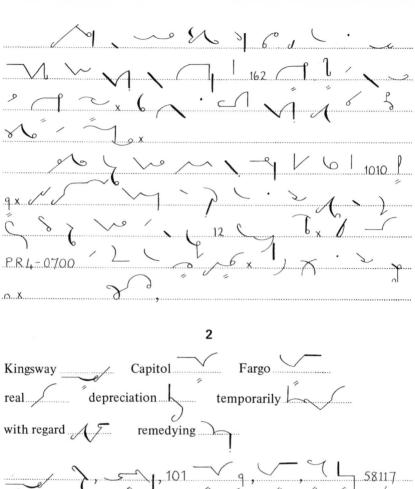

P.R.4.-0700

2

Kingsway _____ Capitol _____ Fargo _____

real _____ depreciation _____ temporarily _____

with regard _____ remedying _____

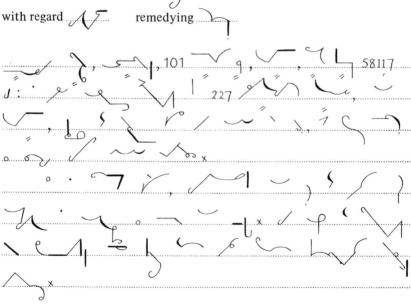

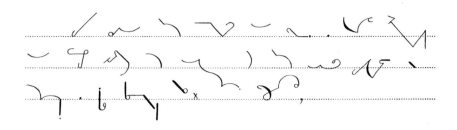

3

Weston 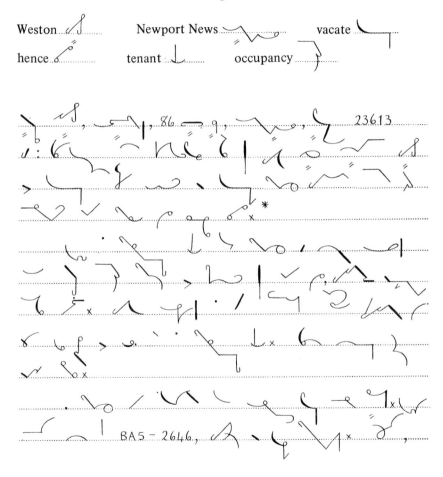 Newport News .... vacate ....

hence .... tenant .... occupancy ....

.... 86 23613

.... BA5 – 2646., ...

* What is the meaning of *six months hence*?

CHALLENGE LETTER

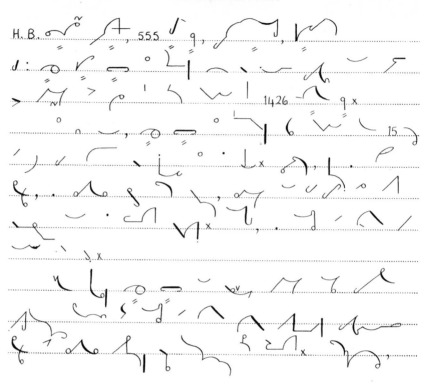

UNIT 5

Key

equipment were worth

SPECIAL OUTLINES

frequent 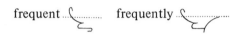 frequently

TRANSCRIPTION POINTER

Here are some additional categories of names which require capitalization:

Associations:	New York Cancer Society
	Phi Beta Kappa
Government branches:	Department of Health
	International Labor Organization
Geographic sites:	the Great Lakes
	the Blue Ridge Mountains
Buildings	the Pan Am Building
	the Municipal Building

1

Oneida laundry residents

neighboring profitably

J.W. , 150 9., , 13227

J.:

355

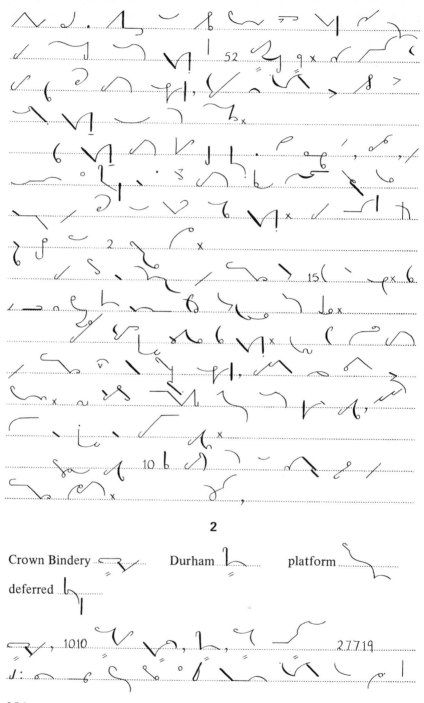

2

Crown Bindery .... Durham .... platform ....

deferred ....

.... 10.10 .... 2.7.7.19

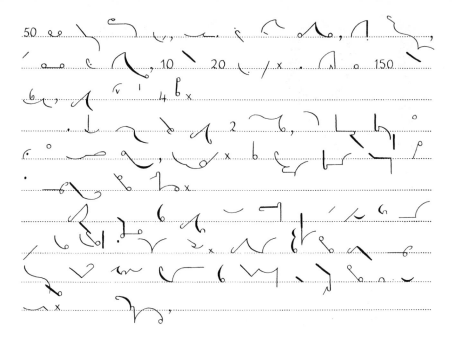

CHALLENGE LETTER

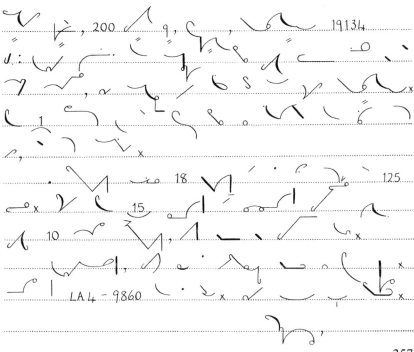

19

Employment

UNIT 1

VOCABULARY BUILDER

Key

concerning contracts recommend magnificent competently

SPECIAL OUTLINES

common ⌐⌐ uncommon ⌐⌐ community ⌐⌐

communicate ⌐⌐

TRANSCRIPTION POINTER

	Abbreviations
Account	A/C, a/c, ac., acct.
Agency	agcy.
Association	assn.
Bank, banking	bk., bkg.

1

Dover ⌐ Delaware ⌐ admission requirements ⌐

liberal ⌐

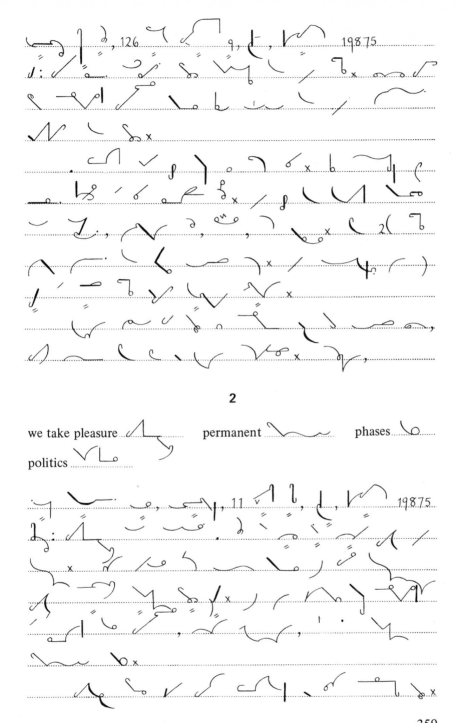

2

we take pleasure .... permanent .... phases ....

politics ....

359

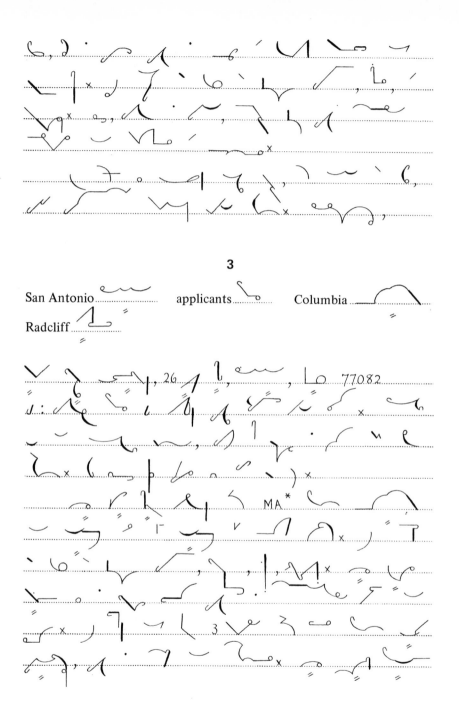

3

San Antonio   applicants   Columbia

Radcliff

26   77082

MA*

3

* MA is the abbreviation for the degree of Master of Arts.

360

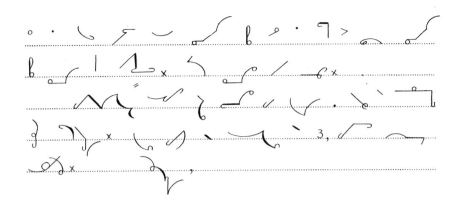

CHALLENGE LETTER

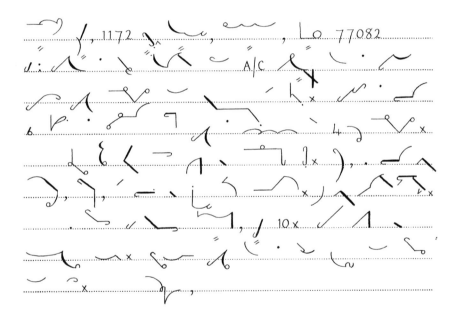

UNIT 2

VOCABULARY BUILDER

Key

commencing instruments conceivable completely complicated
conclusion confidential

SPECIAL OUTLINES

whenever   whatever

Whenever is an adjective or conjunction meaning at any time.
Whatever is an adjective or pronoun meaning anything or any kind.

TRANSCRIPTION POINTER

	Abbreviations
Avenue	Ave.
Street	St.
Road	Rd.
Boulevard	Blvd.
Care of	co. or c/o
North	N.
East	E.
South	S.
West	W.

1

secretarial   skills   meanwhile

musical

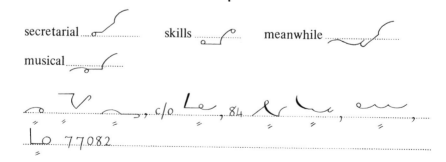

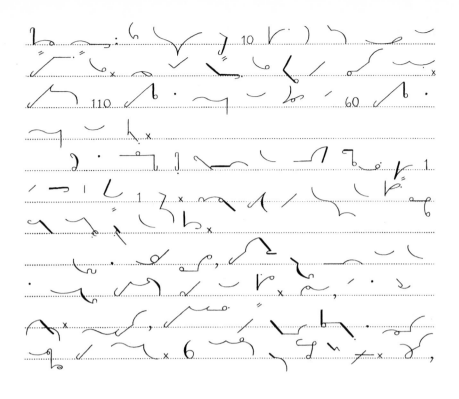

2

Salem ⟨shorthand⟩ Oregon ⟨shorthand⟩ scholastic ⟨shorthand⟩

academic ⟨shorthand⟩

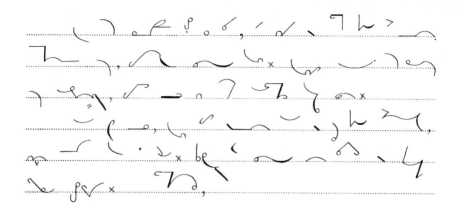

3

résumé ⌒ evaluation ⌣ aptitude ⌐ budget ⟩

CHALLENGE LETTER

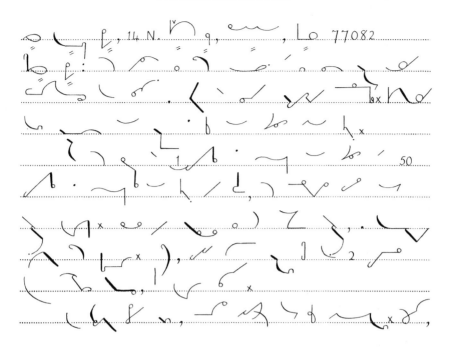

UNIT 3

VOCABULARY BUILDER

Key

consideration contact transfer accompanied connected convenience

SPECIAL OUTLINES

altogether............ together ⌐‿‿‿.

Altogether means wholly.

Together means at one time, as one.

We are not *altogether* convinced that this action is wise.

Let us go to the meeting *together*.

TRANSCRIPTION POINTER

Abbreviations

overcharge   o/c

page, pages   p., pp.

Private Branch Exchange   PBX

  (Switchboard)

1

Portland ⌐⌐ qualifications ⌐‿‿⌐ suited ⌐⌐

relief ⌐⌐

⌐‿ , 65 ⌐ ⌐, ⌐‿, ⌐ 97208

⌐‿ ⌐. ⌐‿ ⌐‿ ⌐ ⌐‿ ⌐

⌐‿ ⌐ ⌐ x

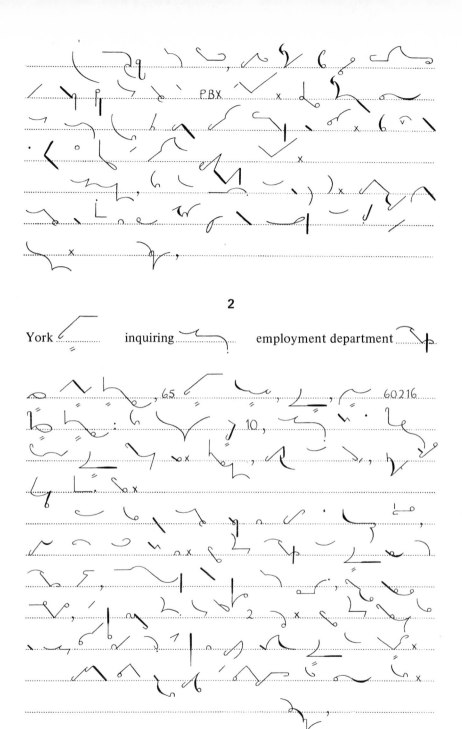

2

York ⌒   inquiring ⌢   employment department ⌢

free-lance 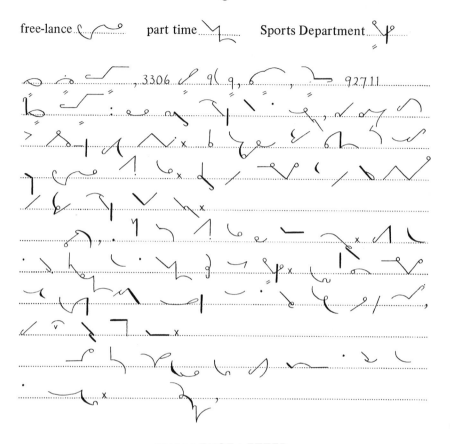 part time   Sports Department

, 3306   , 927.11

CHALLENGE LETTER

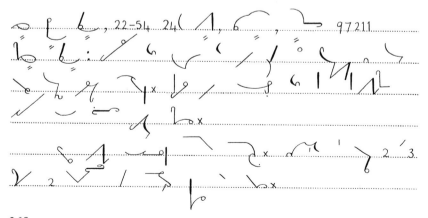

, 22-54   24   , 97.2.11

UNIT 4

VOCABULARY BUILDER

Key

accommodate recommending conduct communications control controllers consumer

SPECIAL OUTLINES

undoubtedly ⌐ in doubt ⌐

no doubt ⌐

TRANSCRIPTION POINTER

	Abbreviations
Company	Co.
Corporation	Corp.
Incorporated	Inc.
Limited*	Ltd.

* *Limited* is a British term, similar to *Incorporated*. The abbreviation, *Ltd.*, is used after a company name just as we use *Inc.*

1

unlimited ⌐ advancement ⌐ judgment ⌐

analyst ⌐

14,205

foremost .... supervisory .... data processing ....

candidate ....

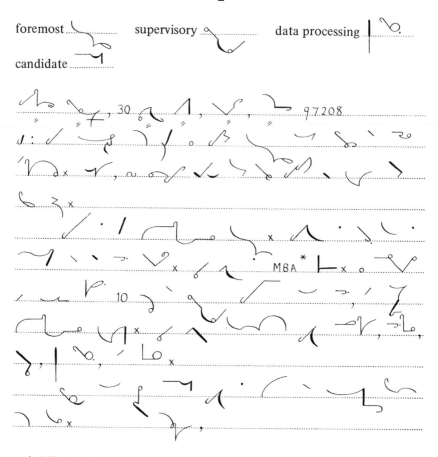

* MBA is the abbreviation for the degree of Master of Business Administration.

CHALLENGE LETTER

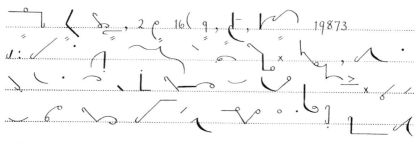

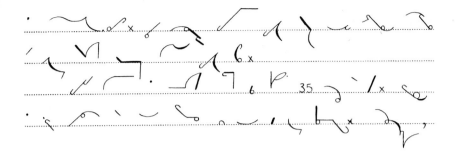

UNIT 5

Key

Transatlantic contracting self-explanatory recognized competitive conductor

SPECIAL OUTLINES

need ‿   needless ⁊

end ‿   endless ⁊

TRANSCRIPTION POINTER

Employment agencies and personnel departments often require a résumé before they will arrange an interview. The purpose of the résumé is to provide a summary of the qualities and qualifications of the applicant.

The résumé should include an outline of the applicant's education, employment experience, and personal and business references. It should also state age, salary requirements, and any other special facts which may help to impress the interviewer.

1

Tracy ⌇   fulfill ⌇   obligation ⌇

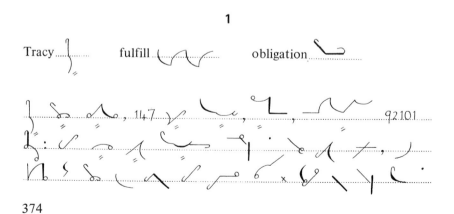

374

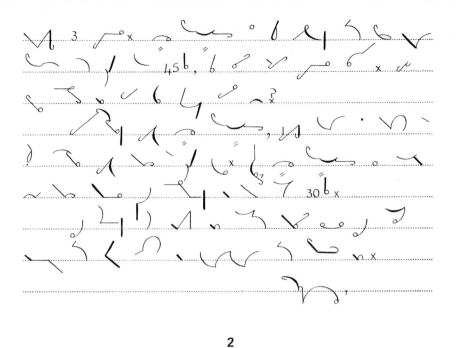

2

apparently ⌄⌄   misunderstood ⌒   it is true

divided

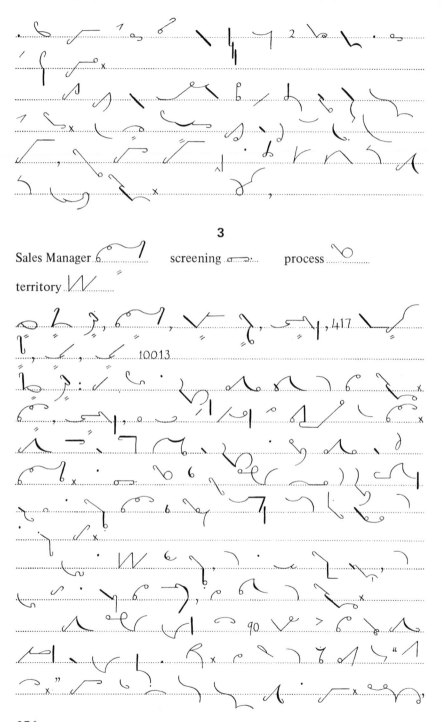

3

Sales Manager screening process

territory

376

CHALLENGE LETTER

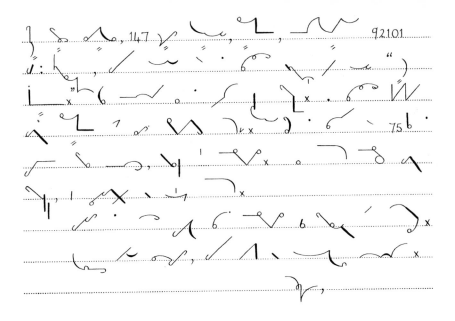

20 Review

UNIT 1

VOCABULARY BUILDER

Key

advertising applying employment working outstanding announcement
Fundamentals opening accounting

SPECIAL OUTLINES

evidently ....L.....   eventually ....L....

evidently (*adverb*) clearly.
eventually (*adverb*) ultimately, finally.

TRANSCRIPTION POINTER

In addition to using a regular check, you should be familiar with these
special types of checks:

Voucher checks: This is similar to an ordinary check, but has a
stub or section on which to indicate for what purpose the check
was issued.

Cashier's checks: This is a check drawn by a bank on its own
funds and is used in situations where a personal check is not
available or acceptable. The bank charges a small fee for issuing a
cashier's check.

378

1

tremendous 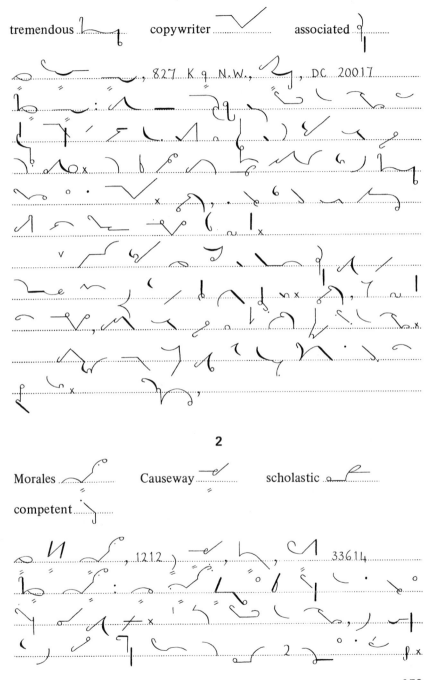 copywriter _____ associated _____

, 827 K q N.W., , DC 20017

2

Morales _____ Causeway _____ scholastic _____

competent _____

, 1212) , , 33614

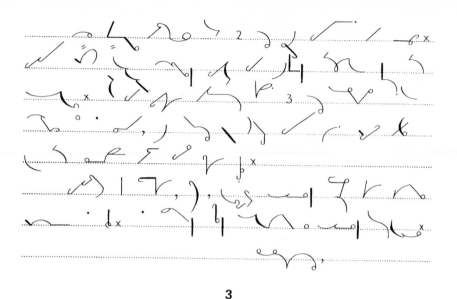

3

Wynn .... numerous .... refresher ....

Supreme Court ....

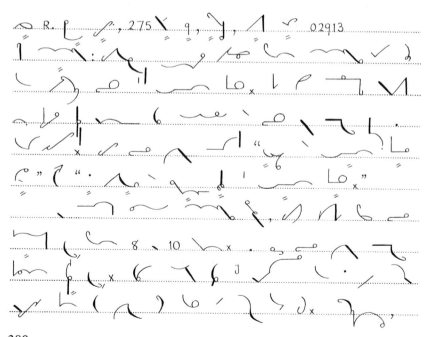

CHALLENGE LETTER

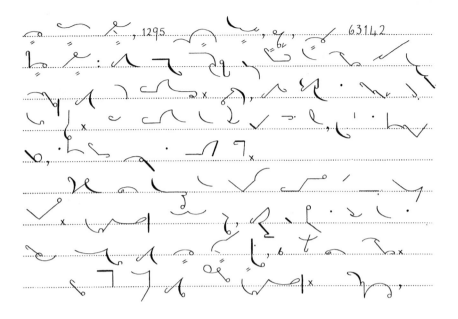

UNIT 2

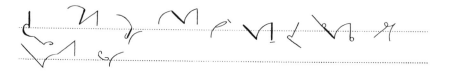

Key

development majority urgently liability listings buildings cheaply possibilities recently popularity friendly

SPECIAL OUTLINES

further ⌒........   farther ⌒........

Further is used to denote quantity or degree.
Farther is used to denote space or distance.

TRANSCRIPTION POINTER

Other special checks include:

Travelers' checks: These checks are issued principally through the American Express Company, telegraph companies, and banks. They are acceptable in distant places where one's personal check might not be honored. To purchase travelers' checks, which come in denominations of $10, $20, $50, and $100, you pay for the face value of the check plus a small service fee.

Express Money Orders: This commercial paper is issued by express companies and is frequently used by people who do not have checking accounts. Express Money Orders are issued in amounts up to $100 and may be endorsed and cashed like checks. The post office, telegraph company, and banks also issue money orders.

382

1

Julian 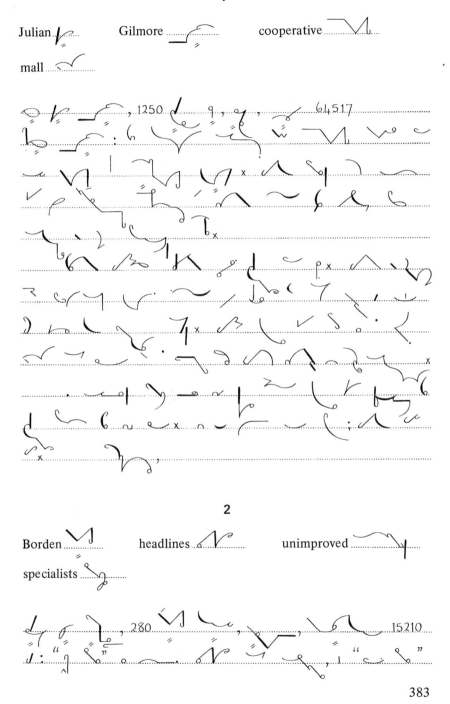 Gilmore cooperative

mall

2

Borden headlines unimproved

specialists

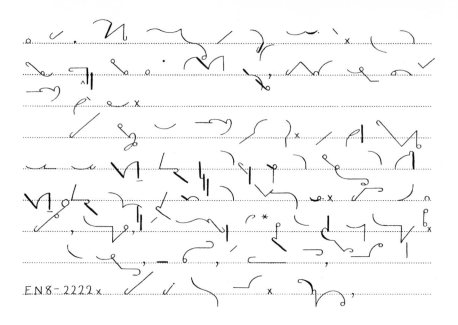

* What is meant by *unimproved land*?

3

O'Brien   freezer   doubled   variety

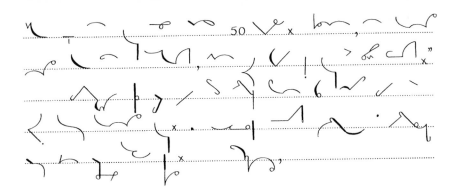

CHALLENGE LETTER

UNIT 3

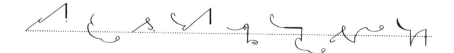

Key

rewarding thoughtfulness responding forward instruments forgetfulness usefulness vitality

SPECIAL OUTLINES

compliment .... complement ....

compliment means a flattering comment; an expression of approval or courtesy.

complement means that which fills up or completes.

The full *complement* of officers and men were saved when the ship went down. Many were *complimented* for bravery.

TRANSCRIPTION POINTER

Reference books are the regular "stock in trade" of a good secretary. You should become familiar with at least one good reference book in each of the following categories:

A dictionary, preferably unabridged
An English style handbook or secretarial handbook
An almanac and an atlas
Local city and telephone directories
The U.S. Official Postal Guide
A hotel directory and a financial directory

1

exposition  anniversary comprehensive

clinics

* An *exposition* is a show or public exhibition.

2

Monroe Edwards Junior

Orchestra Symphony

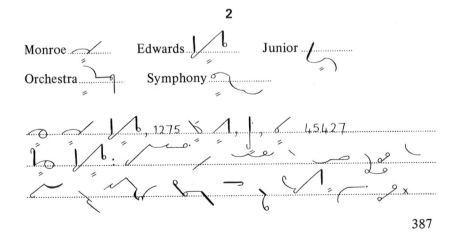

3

Sherman 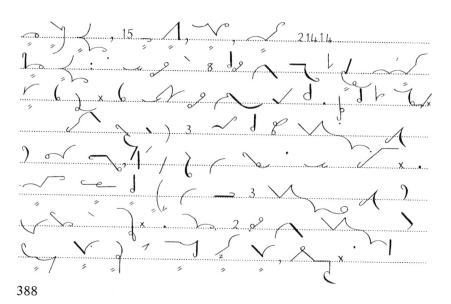 Memorial soloists priority

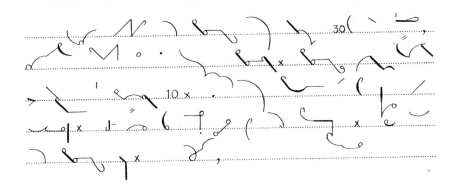

CHALLENGE LETTER

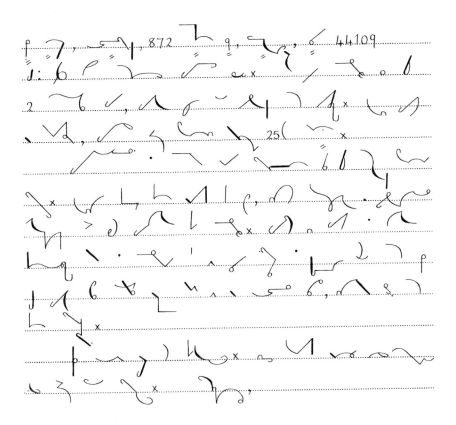

UNIT 4

VOCABULARY BUILDER

Key

citizenship Geological advisability formerly scholarship denying

TRANSCRIPTION POINTER

Here are some abbreviations of foreign words and phrases which are used in English as well:

ad lib.	at one's pleasure
ad val.	according to the value
av., avdp.	avoirdupois (weight)
i.e.	that is
n.b.	note well
op. cit.	in the work cited
prox.	next month
r.s.v.p.	please reply
v.s.	see above

1

Burke .... Bulletins .... forecasts ....

coupon ....

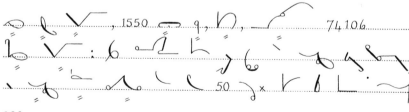

390

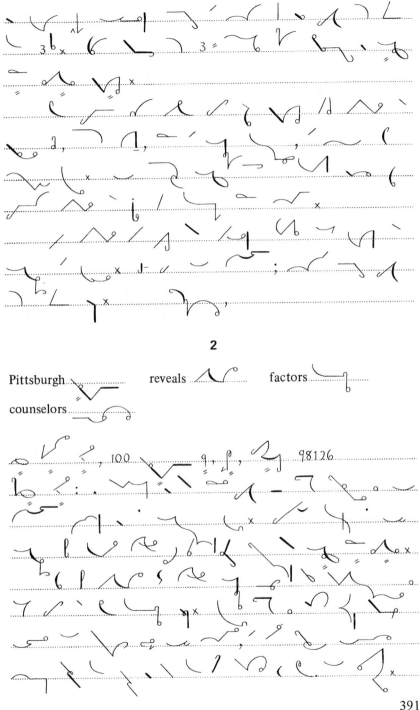

2

Pittsburgh reveals factors

counselors

100 98126

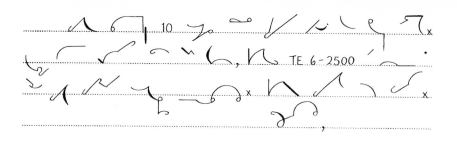

TE 6 – 2500

3

participated  acquisition ⌐e in competition

CHALLENGE LETTER

UNIT 5

VOCABULARY BUILDER

Key

seeking including replacement shortly trying sacrificing

SPECIAL OUTLINES

lend $\mathcal{C}$ loan $\mathcal{C}$ lone $\mathcal{C}$

lend (*verb*) to allow temporary use of.
loan (*noun*) that which is lent; permission to use.
    (*verb*) to lend.
lone (*adjective*) without company; solitary.

TRANSCRIPTION POINTER

Many foreign expressions are used in English speech and writing as if they were part of the idiom of the language. How many of these can you define?

de luxe	table d'hote
bona fide	a la carte
esprit de corps	au gratin
modus operandi	a la king
habeas corpus	hors d'oeuvres
carte blanche	demi-tasse
per capita	parfait

1

rental   distinct   concrete   Chelsea

transaction

394

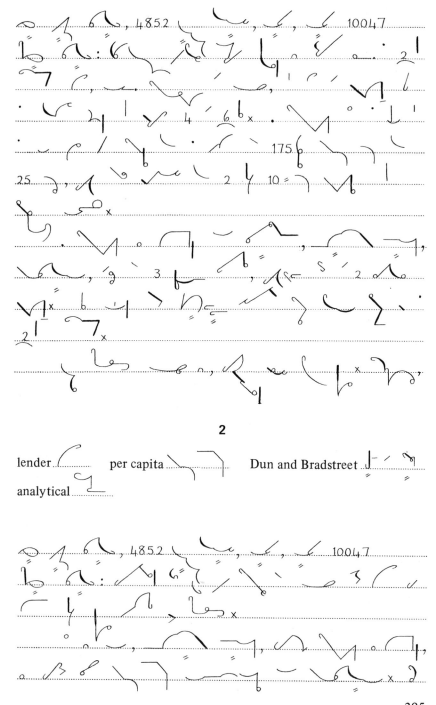

2

lender

per capita

Dun and Bradstreet

analytical

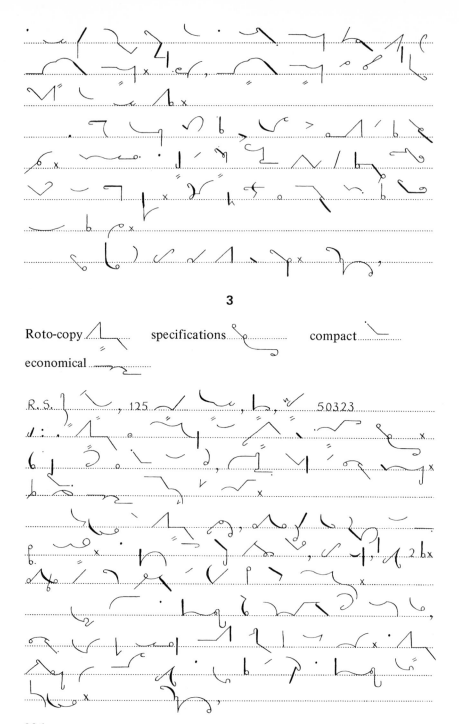

3

Roto-copy ⟋⟍   specifications ⟍   compact ⟍

economical ⟋⟍

R.S. ⟍ , 125 , , 5.03.23

CHALLENGE LETTER